Fascination of Golf

WHITE STAR PUBLISHERS

FORGET YOUR OPPONENTS. ALWAYS

PLAY AGAINST PAR.

Sam Snead

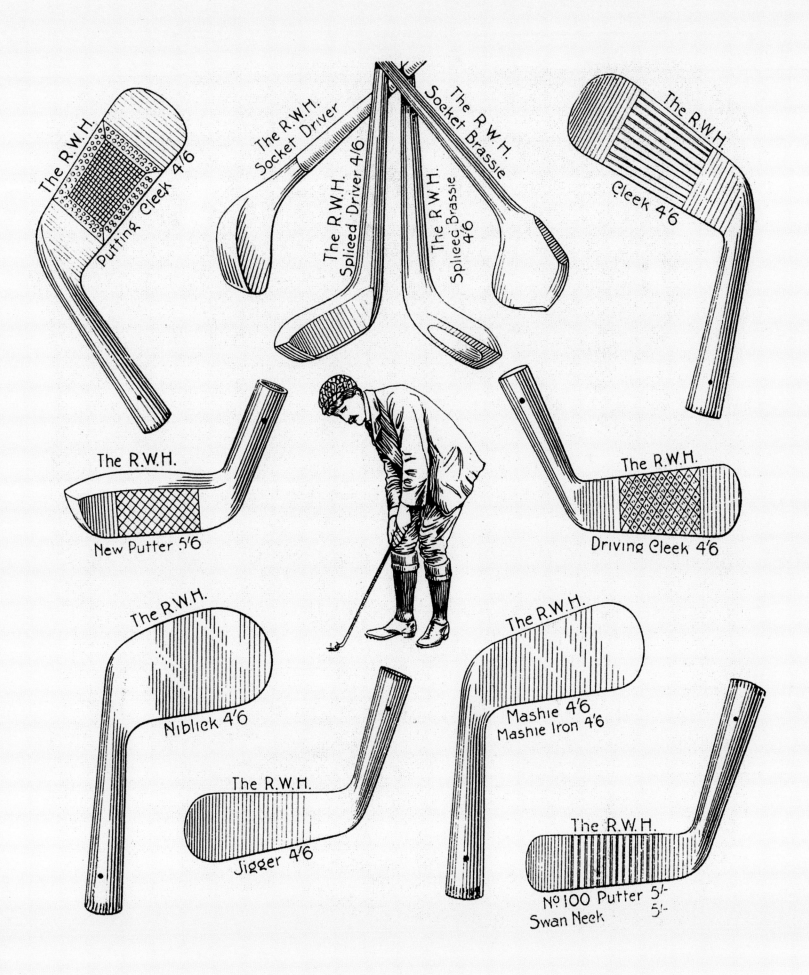

Contents

PREFACE BY Lee Westwood

TEXT BY Maria Pia Gennaro

PROJECT EDITOR Valeria Manferto De Fabianis

EDITORIAL COORDINATION Giorgia Raineri

GRAPHIC DESIGN Paola Piacco

Preface
by Lee Westwood

*W*hen I first discovered that golf was going to be re-introduced to The Olympics, my first question was not will I still be young enough to play in 2016, but simply: Why?

I wasn't sure golf belonged in the Olympics. Watching athletics, swimming, rowing and plenty of other events were what the games were all about to me. Gold medals around the necks of golfers did not hold a particular fascination for me.

And then I started to listen to others and I heard what they said. That the Olympics was the greatest possible way of extending the game's boundaries. It would bring the sport to people who otherwise would not know about it. The greater the interest the greater golf would become with benefits for everybody – not just those who play it both professionally and amateur, but those who promote it, manufacture for it, sponsor it.

I was converted because golf is a game I believe can be enjoyed by all.

Spreading the word about golf is something I see as part of my job to give back to a game that has given me so much. That's why we have opened Lee Westwood golf academies and schools – to give youngsters the chance to be part of golf.

It's also why I agreed to write the introduction to this excellent book by Maria Pia Gennaro which is illustrated by some of the world's best photographers.

The Fascination of Golf produces a wonderful illustration of everything that the game is about and will not be of interest just to the people of Italy where the idea for it originated, but to people throughout the world.

It is a book which lives up to its title – fascinating.

Read it with pleasure and take in the superb images decorating its pages. It will do exactly what The Olympics will add to in 2016 and that is entertain those who are already hooked by golf and attract those who have still to discover its joys.

Lee Westwood

Introduction

I dedicate this book to my son Nicolà.

It is not yet clear whether golf is a sport or a game. For some it is an activity of pure fun and relaxation, while for others it is ther reason for existence. For the latter, golf is a kind of disease. An incurable disease. Once infected, there is no hope. Why? What triggers this compulsion in otherwise "normal" people? The answer lies in the many factors that combine to create the huge, unfathomable, unquenchable charm of golf. They say that beauty fades but fascination remains, and, over the centuries, the allure of golf has grown exponentially. This book examines some key aspects of the attraction of golf, including the many beautiful courses, their evocative images conveying deep feelings even in people who have never played. The message is that golf courses are some of the most beautiful places in the world. Courses, naturally, are not just things of beauty. They are challenges, with every hole and obstacle stimulating the pride and ambition of players. What else can stimulate the competitive spirit in both men and women?

There have been wonderful examples of male and female greatness on the golf course, among both professionals and amateurs, and they have contributed greatly to the development of the game. But there are players whose life stories (and the aura that surrounds them) arouse passions and intrigue, increasing the love for the sport and the number of its followers. Fandom has never failed to be a predominant component of golf, with legions of fans passionately following their heroes in tournaments, breathlessly forming two loving wings along the fairways.

Each tournament, and especially a Major, has its own charm and its appeal is down to the defeats and victories that may have marked its history. Of course, adding a certain panache to this history is the fashion of the game, which deserves a separate discussion, with the clothes of the players over the centuries characterizing fashion itself as yet another unique feature marking golf out as something special.

No other sport requires such strict discipline, both physical and mental. Physical discipline because of the several kilometers an 18-hole course requires players to walk, and because a well-trained physique contributes to a more powerful stroke. Mental discipline because players need to realize that they are not competing against a course or an opponent but against themselves. Any experienced golfer knows exactly what to do, what movements to make and how, and yet, with no apparent explanation, they are often unsuccessful. Discipline and strength of character matter most at this point. Golf is not an immediate sport like tennis: between one stroke and another many long minutes may pass, during which many thoughts may pass through a golfer's mind, distracting them from the game, regardless of the pleasant and often beautiful surroundings of the course. One missed shot can affect a whole round: thinking and rethinking often cause irreparable damage to a score card.

Personal discipline begins with long practice sessions, which every player must undergo to improve technique and learn the rules and the finer points of the game. Golf began as a sport where fair play was the main element, and personal correctness remains the foundation of the game, either in a competitive round or during a practice session. Breaking the rules is like cheating in Solitaire: what satisfaction can you get from a game in which you've cheated?

Golf is one of the most popular sports in the world for many of the above reasons. There are about 70 million practitioners and that number is increasing, even with critics reducing the game to a "five-hour walk on grass, where players repeat an unnatural motion roughly ninety times, all with the aim of putting a ball as small as an apricot in a hole as big as a peach." The increase in popularity has coincided with the evolution of the women's competitive circuit. Like the tennis being played 50 years ago, golf was once considered boring and repetitive. Also like ten-

5 Alone versus the course and themselves. This is the essence of golf.

nis, however, the breakthrough, came with the arrival of players like the Williams sisters, players of such a caliber that they have reduced the gap separating the men's and women's game in terms of performance, power, and entertainment. Today, golf is a real sport at all levels. Both the Sunday player, who practices to distract himself from everyday life, and the senior, who chooses it for the exercise, need to be physically fit to face the long walks implicit in the sport. In recent years, strength training (on a par with psychological training) has become an integral part of the practice of every professional player, with women being just as physically prepared as men.

The men's game, in most cases, is more engaging and exciting, fueled by drives hissing and punching the air (in many cases exceeding 950 ft [290 m]), incredible recovery shots from the rough or from woods where the public can hardly distinguish the player, when, suddenly, a ball lies close to the flag. These shots are beyond the scope of the current women's game. The players, who are less powerful, are nevertheless more consistent and precise. The same holds true on the amateur course, where handicap equals the difference in power between the sexes.

Also, the big-hitting men generally incur more fouls, while, without doubt, women are more accurate. This happens for players of all categories, with power and speed differentiating men's and women's golf. Due to their musculature , men benefit from increased clubhead speed and strength, producing greater distance. Women, for their part, make up for those shortcomings with better rhythm and "timing." When it comes to the psychological side, the advice of

Tiger Woods is of benefit to everyone: "The psychology of golf can be complicated as it does entail mental toughness, self confidence, conquering inner demons, instant recall of past successes and being able to purge failures. It is the game within a game, I developed my mental game early. I cannot overemphasise the importance of you developing yours now."

This book provides equal space for champions and stories, while also focusing on a category of marginal figures that have always been of enormous importance: the caddies. In dictionaries, usually written by people who do not play golf, the word is translated as "boy caddy." The definition, however, is superficial, since there are also "girl caddies." In fact, Henrik Stenson and Nick Faldo have, for years, chosen Fanny Sunesson as their caddy.

Caddies, of course, have much more to do than simply carrying the clubs. They are, in a sense, general factotums, with endless chores both on and off the fairway. A good caddy knows his player and advises, reassures, and instructs him or her about every meter, centimeter and trap of the course. He prepares his player, course after course, with a thorough update at the beginning of every round. It is not just a job and the joy of a caddy can be great. Just think of how happy Billy Foster, Lee Westwood's caddy, was at the end of 2010, when his employer became the world's number one.

Like many other features and elements we've touched upon (and which this book will explore), the caddy has become part of the charm and the lore of golf and has helped develop a real passion for the game, one which continues to grow.

The Fascination With Golf's History

The fascination sparked by an attractive person lies not in those characteristics seen the precise moment of meeting, but in a kind of synthesis of that person's whole being. This synthesis of a person's attractiveness can release a powerful drug that captures the imagination and generates a personal bond. In a similar way the synthesis, or very essence, of golf is almost infinitely large. Consider, for example, the countless tales of confrontations, battles, challenges and struggles, the legends of brave men, talented athletes, rivalries and friendships. Those are tales that can spark the imagination, and, when combined with a myriad of traditions passed down through centuries, can capture your heart. Other aspects, meanwhile, are also important: the competitive spirit, the sweet taste of victory, the sights, the courses and the challenges inherent in the game itself.

Golf, as we know it today, was born of a game played in the kingdom of Fife, on the east coast of Scotland, during the fifteenth century. Players would hit a rock on the sand dunes along the course of a river bank using a stick or a primitive club. However, while many other primitive games involved sticks and a ball, they lacked that essential ingredient unique to golf — a hole. The hole is the target, the goal, the end point, that which gives meaning to the challenge. Some historians believe that the Kolven (or Kolf), from Holland, and the Chole, from Belgium, played a role in the evolution of this primitive game into the one we play today. Regardless of the debate about golf's origins, however, one cannot deny that the game we know today as golf first appeared in Scotland in about 1421.

In its infancy, the country's early history was interwoven with that of golf. Imagine that, at the time, Scotland had to defend itself against an English invasion in the mid-fifteenth century, and yet, nobles often missed military training and archery practice to spend time on the golf course and the football field. Because of this, the Scottish parliament of King James II banned both sports, in 1457. This ban was reaffirmed in 1470 and, again, in 1491, although it was largely ignored by the Scots, who continued to play golf, cheerfully hitting crude balls with strange sticks. Only in February 1502, at the Treaty of Glasgow, did King James IV withdraw the ban, thus allowing the status of golf, and its popularity, to spread rapidly during the rest of the sixteenth century. King Charles I made the game popular in England and it had been Mary, Queen of Scots, a French woman, who introduced the game to France while she was there studying. Mary was also the first woman to play golf in Scotland, which sparked an enormous outcry. This proud queen, who had endured a hard and unfortunate life, had a real passion for the game, a passion that was much criticized especially after she played at St. Andrews only a few days after the death of her second husband, Lord Darnley. The life of Mary, Queen of Scots, began and ended tragically, but it's been said that she did, sometimes, find peace — on the greens.

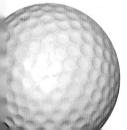

13 Mary, Queen of Scots, was one of the first women to devote herself to golf. Her favorite course was St. Andrews, where she played often, during the winter of 1563.

chapter one

The unfortunate lady has been given credit for one thing however: the term "caddy." In her early twenties she returned to France, where she was educated, and married Francis II. While playing there, she started calling young helpers on the course "cadets," a term which eventually evolved into "caddy."

History also intersected with golf in Leith, near Edinburgh, where, during a game, King Charles I was given the news of the Irish uprising in 1641. Leith was also the site of the first international meeting, in 1682, when the Duke of York and George Patterson, defending the colors of Scotland, beat two English noblemen. The Gentlemen Golfers of Leith were created in 1744, and Leith became the site of an annual competition that offered a silver golf club as a prize. The Gentlemen Golfers of Leith was later renamed the Honourable Company of Edinburgh Golfers, with the first clubhouse being built in 1768. In 1836 the Honourable Company moved to Musselburgh.

The first reference to golf at St. Andrews, however, was in 1552. The clergy allowed public access to the links the following year. In 1754 the St. Andrews Society of Golfers was founded and competed in its own annual tournament and, in 1764, the 18-hole course was built, becoming the standard model for courses around the world. The course today is almost as it was in the days when gentlemen, dressed in a suit and tie, played it: seemingly uncultivated, with only the fairways, greens and tees being maintained. Overall, it required very little maintenance, nature dominating it with all its force, with players having to defy the winds of the North Sea. The Royal & Ancient Golf Club of St. Andrews (R&A) became the worldwide reference body for the publication of rules, royal patronage and the promotion of golf. In this period, golfers began to use the correct clubs and the correct balls. The heads of the clubs were made of beech or from the wood of fruit trees, like apple. Some were hand made out of forged iron, while the shafts were usually made from hazel wood. The balls were made of highly compressed feathers wrapped in hand-sewn leather, which is why, for a long time, golf was only played by rich noblemen: the equipment was very expensive. After 1826, persimmon and hickory were imported from the United States for the production of the club heads and shafts (today, these antiques are highly prized).

William IV bestowed his patronage on the club, honoring it with the title "Royal & Ancient," in 1834, and the new clubhouse, now famous throughout the world, was built in 1854. In 1867, St. Andrews founded a Ladies' Golf Club, which proved to be very successful: in 1893 the number of members had risen to 1312. The entrance fee was seven shillings and six pence and the annual fee two shillings and six pence. These rich ladies made their way to St. Andrews, together, by train, which provided extremely comfortable carriages, dining cars and great service. Thanks to the industrial revolution, by the mid-nineteenth century, railway development in Britain had moved on apace. The development of the railways gave rise to mass tourism. For the first time, even common folk had the opportunity to explore the country on excursions or simply to visit at the weekend. Golf courses began to spring up everywhere and people could enjoy playing a different course every weekend. The trains had luxurious carriages, and each had at least two reserved for ladies only. A singular development in golf came from these ladies, when, still in the middle of the nineteenth century, a group happened to go on summer holiday to Devon, or, more precisely, to Westward Ho! In 1868 they founded the Westward Ho! and North Devon Ladies' Club, with its own nine-hole course, adjacent to the men's course. The total length of the course was 5686 ft (1733 m) (the longest hole was 1138 ft (347 m) and the shortest was 357 ft (109 m), with beautiful greens and numerous obstacles. At its founding, the club had 47 members, all ladies, except for the male teacher who was the only one allowed to give lessons (other men were forbidden to teach women anything with regards to golf).

The British Empire was at its peak during the nineteenth century. The phrase "the sun never sets on the British Empire" was coined to reflect the influence of the Britain around the world. Most of the golf clubs built outside of Britain and United States were in countries that were part of the Commonwealth. The first golf club outside Scotland was founded as the Royal Blackheath near London, in 1766. Some sources, however, indicate that people had been playing there since 1608. The first golf course built outside Britain and the United States was the Bangalore in India, founded in 1820. This was followed by the Royal Calcutta (1829), the Royal Bombay (1842), the Curragh in Ireland (1856), the Pau, in France (1856), the Adelaide in Australia (1870), the Royal Montreal in Canada (1873), the Cape Town in South Africa (1885), St. Andrew's in New York (1888) and the Royal Hong Kong (1889). Some, however, say that the South Carolina Golf Club, in Charleston, preceded them all as it is said to have been founded in 1786.

Beginning in 1848, gutta-percha balls, and clubs with metal or wooden heads, began to be industrially produced, which meant that even the middle classes could afford to play. This encouraged the phenomenal growth in the popularity of golf.

In 1851, the Prestwick Golf Club was founded and was the setting for the 1860 Open Championship, the first Major in history. Here the legend of Old Tom Morris was born, the most influential figure in golf before the twentieth century. The white bearded son of St. Andrews and a pupil of Allan Robertson — known as the first professional in history — won the competition three years in a row, and became a role model for other players. He was not only a great player, but also a valuable greenskeeper, an architect and a club maker. His greatest opponent, however, was his son, Young Tom Morris, who won the event four consecutive times (1869-1872).

Besides a few sponsored competitions, such as the Open Championship, golf professionals earned a living by betting against their opponents, by teaching, by making clubs, or by caddying. The growth of golf as a competitive sport occurred in parallel in Britain, India and in the United States. Receipts from the public were used as prize money for the first time in 1892 in Cambridge, England, and the Amateur Golf Championship in India became the first international golf tournament in 1893.

In 1894, the United States Golf Association (USGA) was established, to regulate the game in the United States and Mexico. In 1900 there were more than 1000 golf courses in the United States, each one following the example of the first American 18-hole course, which had been built in Chicago. The most important American golf courses were, generally, made in landscaped parks, unlike those in Britain. Golf immediately attracted the attention of the media and sponsors, and golf-related business increased dramatically. However, the events still considered most prestigious were those hosted in Britain. Interestingly, amateurs rather than professionals were held in higher esteem by the public.

The dawn of the twentieth century brought with it many technological innovations for golf. One of the first was the Haskell rubber ball, in 1898, which offered an extra flight distance of 66 ft (20 m). A slotted club face was introduced in 1902, and in, 1905, William Taylor invented the dimpled golf ball ('Dympl'). Arthur Knight introduced steel shafts in 1910, though hickory was still widely used for another 25 years.

In the space of a decade, golfers had improved their power and accuracy at very little cost. Around that time, clubs did not have numbers, but names. There was the Baffy (a four/five wood), the driver, the more manageable Brassie (a two wood with a copper sole), the Spoon (a three wood) and the Cleek (a four wood). The classic bag included only the first four woods. These were the tools of the trade for three unmatched characters in the history of golf, three immense players named James Braid, Harry Vardon and John Henry Taylor. The Triumvirate, as they were called, won altogether, 16 Open Championships: a record for three friends that has yet to be matched. Of the three young men — who were all affluent but not wealthy — the quickest to become well known was John Henry Taylor. In 1894, at age 24 he became the first golfer to win the Open Championship when it was held for the first time outside of Scotland, at Sandwich, England. Taylor won the tournament on four subsequent occasions: in 1895, 1900, 1909 and 1913. Then there was Harry Vardon, from Jersey in the Channel Islands, who won the Open six times, in 1896, 1898, 1899, 1903, 1911 and 1914. Scotsman James Braid found success at the Open in 1901, then again in 1905, 1906, 1908 and 1910. In all, five victories. Except for very few cases, it happened that in their time, one of the three won the Open every year. The three were virtually unbeatable. So much so that even when Harry Vardon won the U.S. Open in 1900, behind him in second place, came John Henry Taylor. The scores of the period were not, of course, comparable to those of today but we must take into consideration the equipment and the clothing of the time. Jacket and tie, along with cleat-less shoes certainly did not help stability or allow a major attack on the ball. Even the courses were not as well manicured as they are now, especially at the big events. For example, in 1926 at Scioto (the course where Jack Nicklaus would, later, first come to everyone's attention), many parts of the rough were so high that Bobby Cruickshank's caddy had to drop his golf bag in order to find a ball that had been lost in what seemed like a wheat field. Unfortunately for the caddy, not only did he not find the ball he had been looking for, he couldn't find his bag again afterwards.

All this to say that the Triumvirate, at that time, did not play any better than anyone today: the three were playing a slightly different type of golf. Just think about the ball for instance.

17 Clement Fowler's famous 1913 painting depicting James Braid, Harry Vardon and John Henry Taylor, the Triumvirate that dominated golf during the early twentieth century.

There is a world of difference between the gutta-percha ball of that era and the balls that are used today. Moreover, the three made great use of woods, and the hickory shafts they used required a certain technique and ability. With hickory shafts the swing was essential to golf, as was some creativity, first to imagine the shot, and then to take it. With steel shafts, the shot became a matter of precision and calculation, to say nothing of what's happening today, with equipment made out of much more sophisticated materials. Who was the most important of the three? Historically, the most remembered is Vardon, mostly because of his grip, which has been passed down to modern golfers, completely intact.

James Braid had some difficulties adapting to professional golf: his father, a Scotsman from Fife, had never tried to play and did not understand how anyone would want to make a living as a golfer. In Earlsferry, Scotland, Braid had begun work as an apprentice carpenter in a nearby village, at age 13. He had played the game, but without much conviction. His interest was piqued, however, when he was sent to work in Edinburgh. Once there, he entered, and won, a local tournament. He was about twenty years old. A friend, Ralph Smith, convinced him to go to London. At the time, the Army & Navy department store was looking for carpenters capable of making golf clubs, for which there was a growing demand. James made excellent clubs, for a shilling an hour, and in his spare time, on Sundays, he played more and more, improving each time out. In fact, he ended up creating a swing that Horatio Hutchinson — himself a great amateur, short game master and influential writer — called "Divine Fury." In 1894, James Braid signed up for his first Open Championship.

He was offered a job as a professional in Romford, Essex. From there his career took off. In 1901, at age 31, he managed to win the Open Championship at Muirfield. It was the first of his five wins. At the time, Taylor and Vardon had already won the tournament three times. But Braid quickly made up for lost time and became the first to win it five times. Taylor would later equal this achievement, and Vardon would surpass it with his six victories. At the time, there weren't many big tournaments, and those that did exist were not very frequent.

After his fifth Open win, Braid moved to Walton Heath, Surrey. The rapport that professionals had with their respective clubhouse was different at that time. Despite being one of the founders of the PGA, over which he presided for some years, whenever he arrived at his own club, Braid would enter through the back door and never through the main entrance. He was only, in fact, an honorary member: he was paid for lessons, given lunches (in the kitchen) and he received prizes, which were good but not very substantial. This situation lasted for 25 years. In that time, he helped create some great golf courses, including the King's Course at Gleneagles.

18 Images of James Braid's second Open Championship victory, in 1905. The Scot won the Open five times.

IT IS GOOD SPORTSMANSHIP
TO NOT PICK UP LOST
GOLF BALLS WHILE THEY
ARE STILL ROLLING.

Mark Twain

20 AND **20-21** Illustration by James Braid which, in the opposing photograph, follows the drive of the Argentinean, Jose Jurado, in the 1928 Open Championship at Sandwich.

22-23 James Braid and Ted Ray in a charity match at Sidcup in 1917.

23 James Braid gets out of a bunker during the 1928 Open Championship at Sandwich.

The second man of the Triumvirate, in alphabetical order, was John Henry Taylor, born in north Devon. At age 11, John Henry Taylor left school to work at odd jobs, but that didn't stop him from getting an education, becoming a keen writer and a man of refined manners. In the process he grew up in a hurry. At Westward Ho! he worked as a caddy, a domestic servant in the house of Horatio Hutchinson's father, and he even gave a hand to builders and gardeners. Soon, he had learned everything he needed to know in order to make a living among the workers who maintained the course. He was 17. In the two years that followed he improved his swing, which up to that point had not been great, and become a professional player and greenskeeper at Burnham, Som-

erset. There, in a game that sparked emotions and endless talk, he managed to beat, the then celebrated, Andrew Kirkaldy, who, instead of being annoyed, spoke well of Taylor, helping to make him a professional. In 1893 Taylor's swing sparked a lot of discussion among Scots who saw him in action for the first time at that year's Prestwick Open Championship. The following year, he played in England for the first time, at Sandwich. Taylor had prepared well and, with relative ease, won the first of the sixteen Opens he would win in company with Vardon and Braid. People were bewildered at the sight of this man walking around with a cap on his head, his chin up, and his boots sinking into the mud while he hit the ball straight into the wind like no one they had ever seen before. Of the Triumvirate, John Henry Taylor is perhaps the greatest legend.

24 AND 25 John Henry Taylor won the Claret Jug, the Open Championship trophy, five times. A member of the Triumvirate, Taylor was a man who loved the public. In this photo, he is surrounded by fans in Harrods department store while showing them how he holds a club.

Harry Vardon was born in Grouville on the island of Jersey. He learned to play as a child, using tree branches to improve his swing. In 1887, at age 17, he became an under-gardener for a Major Spofforth. It happened that his new employer was a keen golfer and spotted Harry's ability. He gave him golf balls and golf clubs. At that point, Vardon began studying the grip used by Scottish champion J. E. Laidlay. He would eventually develop his own grip, which is still in use today. When he turned twenty, his brother Tom, a professional at Royal Lytham & St. Annes, convinced him to go to Ripon, in Yorkshire, where he looked for a teacher. The following year he moved to Bury, in Lancashire and, in 1896, he arrived at Ganton, in Yorkshire. There he met John Henry Taylor, who had won the previous two Open Championships. Vardon beat him 8-6. But in the same year, at the Muirfield Open, Vardon and Taylor ended up at par: 316 strokes.

The playoff was over 36 holes: Vardon 157, Taylor 161. Vardon's fame exploded. In 1900 a trip to America was proposed (and subsidized) by a manager who wanted to promote golf in America. There, Vardon won the U.S. Open. He returned wealthy but ill (tuberculosis affected many people at that time), and had to spend some time in a sanatorium to regain his health. In 1914 he won his sixth Open, eighteen years after winning his first. He would compete in America again, but also in Germany and France. His putting would let him down in his later years, but in compensation, he discovered a new technique for hitting off the green. He also played with clubs that were shorter and lighter than usual, and often used by women. In this case, however, they were used by a great man.

26 AND **27** This sequence properly illustrates the Harry Vardon swing.
In the image on the right, Vardon, during an Open Championship, is credited with first use of the grip still used by most golfers today.

The Professional Golfers' Association of America (PGA) was formed in 1916 and initially had only a winter 'circuit'. Eventually, in 1944, the circuit would expand to become all season and consist of 22 events. In 1921, the R&A had imposed size and weight limits on golf balls, that imposition started a 30-year dispute between European and Commonwealth countries, and the United States (regulated by the USGA). Most of the differences were resolved by 1951, when both parties agreed to a common set of rules. However, the question of the size of the golf ball was not resolved until much later — 1988! Today, worldwide golf is regulated jointly by the R&A and the USGA, with rules modified every four years.

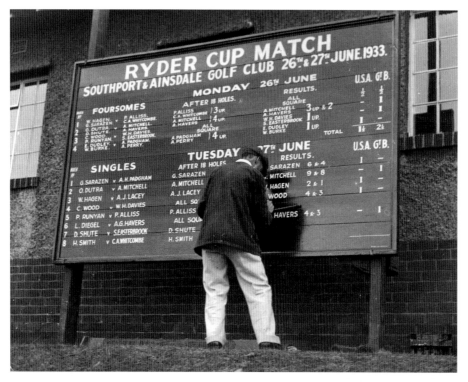

The rift between the two golfing powers, America and Britain, was accompanied by the introduction of the Ryder Cup in 1927, a competition between the best professionals from both countries. Initially, the Europeans were represented only by golfers from Britain and Ireland. The Americans, with their wealth of talent, won every meeting between 1935 and 1985, with the exceptions of 1929 and 1957. Only since 1979 have players from outside the British Isles been allowed to play as part of the European team, and since then, the competition has become truly competitive.

28 The leader board at the 1933 Ryder Cup, the meeting between the United States and Great Britain & Ireland, played at Southport.

28-29 The victorious United States team at the 1927 Ryder Cup. At the center is team captain Walter Hagen.

30-31 Englishman Henry Cotton congratulates American Walter Hagen, who beat the course record at Muirfield during the Open Championship.

31 A large crowd watches Henry Cotton escape from a bunker at the 1500 Guineas Southport-Dunlop Professional Golf Tournament.

Perhaps the most famous player in the pre-war period was the American Bobby Jones: well read, educated — he had earned degrees in law and engineering — and refined, he remained an amateur all his life despite being considered the greatest player ever, before Tiger Woods stepped on the scene. Among his many achievements was his victory at the original Grand Slam in 1930, at age 28. After he retired, he was rich enough to create, almost as a whim, the Augusta National course, where, since 1934, the Masters have been played in his honor. This event had been designed, by Jones himself, as a way for him to meet professional old friends. Other eminent players were Sir Henry Cotton, who won the Open Championship in 1936, for the third consecutive

time, and Walter Hagen who won four Opens, as well as two U.S. Opens and three PGA Championships. Hagen redefined the figure of the professional at clubhouses. Early in Hagen's career, it was not uncommon for golf clubs to refuse clubhouse entry for professional golfers. On one occasion Hagen discovered that he had been denied entry to the restaurant and the locker rooms. In response, he hired a limousine, parked it near the clubhouse, and used it his changing room. On another occasion he gave his £100 prize money to his 16 year old caddy, as a tip. Elegant and with an over the top personality, he became the terror not only of tailors, shoe makers and shirt makers, but also of chefs and sommeliers. Hagen had not been born wealthy, and he loved money for the comfort, the elegance and the beautiful women that it could bring him. He also enjoyed the many trips it allowed him to take, earning victories in France, England, Belgium and Canada. Hagen was also the heart and soul of the Ryder Cup team at the time, serving as team captain for the first six editions.

Other great golfers of the time included Joyce Wethered, who won the Ladies Championship five times in a row in the 1920s, and Glenna Collett Vare, who won her sixth Women's U.S. Amateur tournament in 1935.

Many say that American golf was created by the hands of John Reid, a Scotsman who had emigrated, with his wife, to the United States. Organizing three holes on a lawn behind his house in Yonkers (New York), he had begun playing golf with his wife and two friends, in 1899.

In reality, Miss Florence Boit had just as big a part to play in the evolution of golf stateside, as she had returned from a vacation in Pau, France (where the first golf club in continental Europe had been created) seven years earlier, bringing back golfing equipment and a passion for the game. Her story, however, is part of a greater tale, which started even earlier.

In 1808, Spain rebelled against French occupation. In 1812, the Duke of Wellington, in the war of liberation (The Peninsular War), defeated the French, forcing France to withdraw from Spain. Part of Wellington's army was a group of Scottish fusiliers, who, when injured, were sent to convalesce in Pau. Once rehabilitated, many did not wish to fight again, and they resumed the peacetime habits of home, including the playing of golf. Recruits were not lacking, and, in 1856, the Pau Golf Club was born, supported by many British travelers vacationing there, attracted by the beauty of the Pyrenees. From the United States came the aforementioned Florence Boit, who quickly became impassioned by the game. When Florence returned home, she discovered that, in her hometown of Boston, no one knew anything about golf. So, she started to tell people about it, before giving a demonstration of the game to Laurence Curtis at the Country Club in Brookline, Massachusetts. Curtis was part of the management board and she convinced the club to spend $50 to build the first nine holes. The ladies liked the game so much that by the following year, a nine-hole course had been opened on the beautiful beaches of Shinnekock in Southampton, for ladies only. Very stylish, the course dictated tastes for the whole of the east coast, and inspired another group of ladies in Morristown, New Jersey to open their very own seven-hole course in 1894, the first ladies only golf club. They also organized a tournament.

32 Joyce Wethered receives the trophy for the Ladies Open Amateur Championship from the captain of St. Andrews, Colonel Skene Moncrieff.

34-35 AND 35 The unbeatable amateur golfer Joyce Wethered had very few rivals in the 1920s. In the image on the right she is seen
at the end of an encounter with Madame Lacoste, which she won 5-4.

DON'T PLAY TOO MUCH GOLF.

TWO ROUNDS A DAY ARE PLENTY.

Harry Vardon

36-37 Joyce Wethered guides the audience through the Swilcan Bridge at St. Andrews during the Ladies Open Amateur Championship.

Men were limited to watching, and they began to worry. They would have preferred that their wives and daughters remain at home or simply rested on the verandas of the Country Club. As more and more golf courses were created, men slowly took over, gradually reducing ladies' admission times. In certain cases, they even refused entry to ladies altogether. But these actions had their consequences. In the summer, on the east coast, ladies continued to learn the game, constantly practicing and organizing frequent tournaments. By doing so, a tradition of ladies amateur play began, and has continued to this day, throughout the world. In 1900, the Curtis sisters of Manchester, Massachusetts, Harriot (22) and Margaret (20), were excellent golfers, but also, crucially, very wealthy. On 25 May 1905, both arrived at the Royal Cromer (a private club, founded in 1888, in Norwich, England) as part of a group of eight American ladies who had come to England to compete with the most talented English players. The English won handily. Nevertheless, the two Curtis girls had fun, so much so that they began to dream up an event that would bring together golfers from different countries. The Curtis Cup would come to life in 1932, as a biennial competition that saw English and American competitors vying for a small trophy — a beautiful silver rose bowl designed by Paul Revere. This cup would become the symbol of the greatest sportsmanship and best golf on both sides of the Atlantic. In the meantime, each of the two sisters had won the Women's U.S. Amateur tournament, with Harriot winning the first in 1906. In 1907, the incredible happened: Harriot and Margaret competed against each other in the final. Margaret won, and she repeated the feat in 1911 and 1912. In all, Margaret played the tournament 25 times, the first in 1897. Fifty years later, she would compete in the tournament again at the age of 65, bowing out two years later, in 1949.

The Ladies PGA was formed in 1951 (the European version in 1988) and replaced the Women's Professional Golf Association. The first Women's Open was held in 1946 and was won by Patty Berg. Perhaps the greatest woman golfer of the time was Mildred 'Babe' Didrikson Zaharias, who won the Women's U.S. Amateur Championship in 1946, the Women's British Amateur Championship in 1947 and Women's U.S. Open Championship in 1948, 1950 and 1954. If that were not enough, she had devoted herself to golf after retiring from athletics having won three Olympic medals and set numerous world records.

38 Harriot Curtis in action. With her sister Margaret, she gave the cup and their name to the biennial meeting between the United States and Great Britain.

40-41 The American team that won the 1936 Curtis Cup against their British rivals.

The Augusta National opened in April 1933. The first Masters was played in 1934 and was won by Horton Smith. Gary Player from South Africa broke the American monopoly of the event in 1961. When the Second World War began in 1939, competitions in Britain had been largely suspended. The War Department earmarked all supplies of rubber and metal for the war and conscripted all men of fighting age. The Americans followed suit when they too went to war in 1942.

After the war, the majority of professionals chose to compete exclusively in America because of the more substantial prizes. Following this, the R&A increased the prize money for the Open Championship to encourage the best players to compete in Europe.

Every era has its champions. One of the greatest personalities in the world of golf was Ben Hogan, born in Stephenville, Texas, in 1912. Gene Sarazen, who saw Harry Vardon play, but who lived long enough to follow, one by one, all the other greats up to Tony Jacklin, said in a famous interview: "Nobody has ever been able to hit the flag like Ben Hogan." A big man? Quite the contrary. In 1940, when he was top of the Money List, Ben Hogan weighed 136 pounds.

Since 1929 metal shafts had been allowed. Clubs, therefore, weighed more, and, since they were largely handmade, there were great differences between them. To better understand the level of Ben Hogan, one need only cite his two victories of 1946 and 1948 at the U.S. PGA. But there were also the U.S. Opens in 1948, 1950, 1951 and 1953 and the two Masters in 1951 and 1953. In 1953, he not only won the last of his four U.S. Opens, but also his second Masters, and, at Carnoustie in Scotland, he won the Open Championship to the applause of spectators and players alike. It is worth mentioning that at the 1953 Open Championship, Ben Hogan had to play (for the first time in competition) with the small ball, that was used in Europe. Between 1938 and 1959, he won 57 rounds on the American Tour.

Ben Hogan is one of five golfers who have won all four Grand Slam events, along with Jack Nicklaus, Gary Player, Gene Sarazen and Tiger Woods.

42-43 The great Ben Hogan studying the line of a putt.

The Grand Slam is made up of the U.S. Open, the PGA Championship, the Masters and the British Open Championship. The real, completely unbeatable grand slam, has only been achieved once, in 1930, by Bobby Jones, who, in the same year, won the two Opens and the two Amateur championships in Britain and the US. The life of Ben Hogan, however, would soon take an extraordinary turn that would keep him dangling perilously between life and death. On 2 February 1949, in Texas, Ben Hogan's car was totally destroyed in a collision with a 10-ton Greyhound bus. Hogan was seriously injured and fractured vertebrae, ribs, his pelvis and hip. These injuries healed, but a consequential blood clot proved to be a bigger problem. To prevent it from reaching his heart, doctors had to intervene, and performed a daring operation to block the veins in his legs, impeding the clot's movement.

Everyone was convinced that Hogan would never play golf again. To prove everyone wrong, a month after the last operation in El Paso, and still with an obvious and painful limp, he embarked for Ganton, in Yorkshire, ready to do his job as team captain of the American team in the 1949 Ryder Cup. The Americans won 7-5. No one thought they would see him again on the first tee of any course. How wrong had been. He now walked with difficulty but took part in six minor competitions before signing up for the 1950 U.S. Open. Less than 16 months after the accident, in Merion, just outside Philadelphia, he was at the top of his game again.

Never without his white cap, Ben Hogan became one of the most popular figures in golf. He was a great coach and, in 1948, he published a book on the game that has become a golfing classic. In 1954, he founded the Ben Hogan Co., which produced golf clubs. In 1960 he sold the company, but still kept an interest in the business, most especially in the development of the most popular products (balls and clubs).

44 A forerunner of modern fittings, Ben Hogan took personal care of his clubs.

46 The leader board at the 1961 Masters. Studying it is "The King," Arnold Palmer.

The 1960s brought us something special in the guise of Arnold Palmer, Jack Nicklaus and Gary Player — the Modern Triumvirate that dominated the game for a long time from 1960 onwards, winning almost all of the major events around the world and competing in international matches. Nicklaus for example, still boasts the unbeaten record of four U.S. Opens, six Masters, five PGA Championships and three Open Championships. While the pre-war period can be regarded as the era of women's liberation, both socially and in golf, the 1960s brought with them the fight against racial discrimination. In 1961, the PGA abolished racial discrimination: Charlie Sifford became the first black golfer to compete in a tournament on the PGA Tour and, in 1975, Lee Elder became the first black golfer to win the Masters. Although there were other changes, as recently as 1990, when the PGA introduced further measures to end racial discrimination, some clubs, particularly Cypress Point, withdrew from the Tour.The Americans and the South African Gary Player dominated golf in the 1970s. Only when Severiano Ballesteros won the 1979 Open Championship and the 1980 Masters, did the pendulum swing in favor of the Europeans. Sandy Lyle, Nick Faldo and Colin Montgomerie's competitive presence restored Britain to world class parity. Individual success was tied to team success, when the Europeans, led by Tony Jacklin, won the 1985 Ryder Cup, ending a run of American dominance. The Solheim Cup, a female version of the Ryder Cup, was launched in 1990 and the following year, a European, Ian Woosnam, was at the top of the world rankings. European golf has grown visibly with the help of Ken Schofield, the supreme head of the European Tour, and his successor in the new century, George O'Grady. At the same time prize money has increased from year to year, reaching many millions of dollars, much of which has been won by the recent king of the links, Eldrick Tont 'Tiger' Woods.

At the same time, equipment has also evolved: manufacturers have designed new clubs, woods and putters using the very latest materials. These new materials have radically changed the game by allowing players to drive previously unheard of distances, forcing courses to be redesigned in some cases, incapable as they are, of withstanding the advent of new techniques, new tools and the march of time.

48-49 Arnold Palmer celebrates a putt that won him the 1964 Masters.

The Modern Triumvirate

49 A young Gary Player jokingly observes
the flight of the ball. The South African champion
dominated golf in the 1960s and 1970s along
with Arnold Palmer and Jack Nicklaus, below, getting
out of a bunker.

I NEVER WANTED

TO BE A MILLIONAIRE.

I JUST WANTED

TO LIVE LIKE ONE.

Walter Hagen

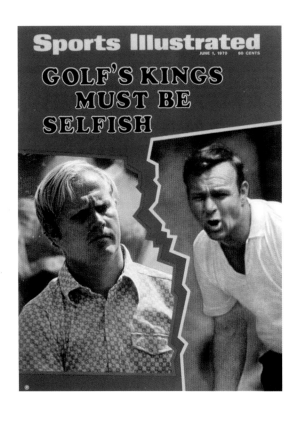

50 The rivalry between Palmer and Nicklaus was enhanced by this *Sports Illustrated* cover.

Sports Illustrated

3 OWN STORY
A LIFELONG SILENCE

A LIFELONG SILENCE

strated

JUNE 10, 1968   40 CENTS

WHO RULES THE GAME?   CHAMPION JACK NICKLAUS

50-51 During the presentation of the U.S. Open, *Sports Illustrated* caught the "Golden Bear" engaged in an unusual game of pinball.

Golf today

52 Nick Faldo, knighted for sporting achievement, has won six Major titles, three Masters and many Open Championships.

53 The leap of joy after Sandy Lyle hit the target and won the 1988 World Matchplay Championship at Wentworth.

54 Severiano Ballesteros marked a new era with his charisma, acrobatic play and presence on the course.

55 Aside from a clothing line logo, this gesture
from Ballesteros became the symbol
for triumph.

56 Colin Montgomerie, who has won the European Order of Merit seven times, is a controversial figure known for having a very difficult character.

56-57 Montgomerie in action at Augusta. "Monty" is one of the best players in the world to have never won a Major.

ONE THING ABOUT
GOLF IS YOU DON'T
KNOW WHY YOU PLAY
BAD AND WHY YOU
PLAY GOOD.

George Archer

58 The man who changed golf: this is one
of the first of thousands of covers devoted
to the phenomenon of Tiger Woods.

58-59 From 1997 to the end of 2009, Tiger Woods broke record after record, winning 14 Major titles.

The Fascination with Golf's Fashion

*D*ressing with style means also being able to appreciate style. When you look at the bright clothing worn by professionals today, it is worth remembering that in the very first Open Championship, all eight competitors wore identical green and white jackets, provided by a local company "in order to beautify their appearance."

Golf has a reputation for being the sport with the worst dressed athletes in the world. Although the sport itself is recognized as one of the most elegant, most golfers seem willing to offset their experience with totally inappropriate clothing for the big tournaments.

Golfers of earlier times did not put any special effort into finding appropriate clothing for their sport. The original 'uniform' most probably consisted of a kilt supplemented by animal skins, as worn by Scottish shepherds who were the first players of the game. Over time, European nobility developed a fondness for golf, and its apparel underwent changes reflecting the popular fashion among those who played more frequently. When it came to men's fashion, the first major changes involved pants. Men, at the time, were tired of wide breeches and shorts, which were originally worn as under garments. Newer styles were still large, but were held in place below the knee with ribbon. Gradually, the rest of the leg became more close-fitting and both the flap and the knee were fastened with the aid of buttons.

Waistcoats became tighter and were fastened from the waist. Most often, they were paired with similar tuxedo jackets and woolen ties.

Towards the end of the nineteenth century the edges of men's pants grew longer, and long pants became a trend in all sectors of society. Rather than embrace this trend, golfers decided to mask it by tucking the bottom of their pants into long socks. In the nineteenth century, it was also not unusual to see golfers wearing a hat. Few golfers had the courage to take off their heavy jackets and ties, even in the warmest of weather.

The image of Allan Robertson, considered by many to be the father of professional golf, attired in heavy tweed, is a typical example of men's clothing from the nineteenth century. Long, wide pants and loose, comfortable, shirts and jackets with huge slightly misshapen pockets, were fashionable, as were V-neck shirts and bow ties, which were de rigueur even in the warmest of weather.

chapter two

61 This manifesto of the late nineteenth century was created by Maxfield Parrish, and reproduced on the cover of *Harper's Weekly*. Style, class and elegance were the hallmarks of the late nineteenth century. A period in which men wore slender, tailored clothes, with a shirt and the ever-present bow tie.

HARPER'S WEEKLY

NATIONAL AUTHORITY ON AMATEUR SPORT

The period between 1800 and 1830 was characterized by "dandy fashion," a style epitomized by George Brummell, who gained notoriety with his "English style," but in reality created nothing really new.

Frills were reduced to a minimum in this period and more attention was paid to the cut and the fabric detailing. The jacket, with a sort of coat-tail, was double-breasted and high-waisted, being short at the front and long at the back, with tails to the knee. The neck was very tall, and it fell on the shoulders in two big lapels, which were foldable thanks to buttons. More often than not, however, they were left open to show the formidable white tie.

Vests were short and straight-layered, single or double-breasted, with a small straight neck and two huge lapels, which often covered the jacket. After 1830 the lapels of the jacket disappeared and the neck increased in height, without, however, exceeding the jacket. Pants of the era could be very loose or much tighter than those of the past. The latter almost resembled long underwear, stopping at the ankles and leaving only low-cut shoes or boots exposed, like so-called "hussar pants." Looser pants of the day usually came with three or four fastening clips. Long enough to reach the feet, they were slightly folded, but could also be stuffed into a pair of calf-high boots.

At the beginning of the nineteenth century, colors became more sober, reflecting autumn. These same colors remain in the classic male wardrobe of today, including black, blue (light or dark), bottle green, brown, beige and iron gray.

The most essential item of clothing, however, was the shirt. During the nineteenth century the collar rose considerably and was left either soft and folded, or heavily starched to give the tie a firm backing. This also guaranteed the wearer a more confident and "convenient" posture for the golf course.

Around 1830, male fashion went through a change, and many styles were cleaned up and much more refined compared to the more creased style preferred in the early years of the century. The sidecut at the waist became evident, providing smoother and more solid volumes, with little or no sleeve and pleated folds. The man of the 1830s preferred color on his tie and vest. In golf, however, he did not skimp on the plaid pants, which were much looser than the tighter designs of earlier years. The big fashion breakthrough, however, came in the mid-nineteenth century, with the introduction the short, wide, jacket which would find a role in both general and sporting attire.

63 Horatio Hutchinson, who won the British Amateur Championship at St. Andrews in 1886, in an image from 1890. Characteristic of the era are the trousers tucked into socks and the short, wide jackets, which would become a symbol of distinctive elegance.

THE LADIES' WORLD

SEPTEMBER, 1901

FIVE
CENTS

S. H. MOORE & CO., NEW YORK

Women's golf began to develop in the mid-nineteenth century when some ladies, during a hot summer season, went on holiday to Devon and, in particular, to Westward Ho!, a seaside resort on the Atlantic touched by the Gulf Stream. The ladies arrived by train, preceded by trunks suitable for storing their fine clothes. A job that no longer exists today is that of the trunk packer, who had to be able to accommodate huge skirts without creasing them. The most famous packer was a Frenchman, the favorite of Empress Eugenie whom she used whenever she traveled to the house in Biarritz that her husband Napoleon III had given her. His name was Louis Vuitton and, by filling these trunks for a living, he managed, as he was also a skilled craftsman, to eventually produce trunks that were lighter and more sound. He would become famous.

It was right in the heart of Devon that these ladies discovered golf, and not only as a sport for the holidays. Since the beginning of the twentieth century, golf clubs for ladies began to spread, and with them, came carefully studied fashion, including blouses that allowed the freedom of movement necessary for an effective swing. Skirts were long, to the feet, and players wore hats with pom-poms.

Women's golf took hold in America thanks to the first real champion, sixteen year old Beatrix Hoyt, who won the women's national title in 1897 finishing two rounds at Shinnecock in under 80 shots. Hoyt played with a beautiful long skirt, to the foot, a lace blouse and a white ribbon in her hair. She won the Women's U.S. Amateur title three times in a row. Her nearest competitor in those years was never closer than six strokes. This winning streak was interrupted in 1900 with a defeat inflicted by Margaret Curtis. Beatrix Hoyt retired from competition at age 20. Her record as the youngest Women's Amateur winner remained unbeaten until 1971.

64 This cover of the most popular women's magazine in the United States is dedicated to women's golf.

GOLF IS LIKE A LOVE AFFAIR. IF YOU DON'T TAKE IT SERIOUSLY, IT'S NO
FUN. IF YOU DO TAKE IT SERIOUSLY, IT BREAKS YOUR HEART.
Arthur Daley

66 The cover of the official magazine of the United
States Golf Association, the organization that runs U.S.
golf with the PGA.

67 The Ledger Monthly was a monthly American
magazine for families that was instructive and famous for
illustrations by the best artists of the time.

THE LEDGER MONTHLY

NEW YORK MAY 1899

The early years of the twentieth century are known as the Belle Epoque. A period of optimism and cheerfulness in which major advances in science and industry, represented by the great Universal Exposition in Paris in 1900, had spread great confidence for the future.

Men's fashion in the early twentieth century saw little change compared to women's fashion. The unquestioned arbiter of elegance was King Edward VII of England, who emphasized an often brightly colored vest, and golfers followed these dictats until the end of World War II when, finally, this was abolished in golf. The shirts of the day were strictly white, with interchangeable necks and cuffs. Collars were most usually "dressed" with a tie.

Liberalization during the 1920s brought some changes in clothing fashion for both genders. Men lost the bulkiest item in their wardrobe: the formal jacket. Ties, however, remained and they replaced the bow tie. The habit of tucking pants inside long socks also persisted. In this period the V-neck shirt became very popular. Meanwhile, sweaters took the place of vests, which had hindered movement. These sweaters were usually in solid colors with contrasting edges, or in bright colors with geometric designs. Some of the most audacious players wore brightly-patterned socks, and ended up looking like clowns.

Walter Hagen popularized the widespread use of colorful clothing on fairways. Just imagine the effect that he created with his colored breeches, two-tone undershirts and shoes, while other competitors were dressed in brown and gray! In his first U.S. Open, in 1913, Hagen wore a checkered black and white cap, a silk shirt with large red and blue lines, a red scarf and white shoes with red soles. He later changed his style, becoming very demanding and extremely refined, a real terror for tailors, shoemakers, shirt makers, chefs, maître d's and sommeliers.

69 During the Belle Epoque, bright and cheerful colors prevailed, but a looser shirt that did not impede movements had not yet appeared.

70 The four champions Bobby Jones, Jess Sweetser,
Gene Sarazen and Walter Hagen (left) in the 1920s.
Men were liberated from the constraints of jackets,
replacing them with more comfortable V-neck sweaters
worn over shirts.

71 Walter Hagen competing in the 1920 U.S. Open
at the Winged Foot Golf.

72 South African champion Bobby Locke during the 1953 Open Championship at Carnoustie.

73 Among Clark Gable's favorite courses was Cypress Point. On vacation, the actor divided his time between golf and fishing.

74 British champion Henry Cotton was chosen as the face of the new Lotus cleats.

74-75 American Lloyd Mangrum gets out of a bunker during the 1952 Masters at Augusta.

With the Belle Epoque, a period in which fashion followed the opulence of the ballroom, gala dinners and aristocratic residences, the fashion of needing to have clothes for different times of the day arose. Women wore dresses that emphasized femininity, with skirts that widened at the bottom, bodices that were tight at the back and puffed at the chest, and made extensive use of belts, to further increase the curved effect. Clothes for sport, in soft light fabrics, had high lace collars and soft pastel colors, and, at the feet, soft boots in patent leather.

Since 1910, a new style had arisen that completely broke with previous fashions: a new straight, slender, design with long, tight, skirts (which made walking difficult). Life was no longer the focal point of female fashion design, which gave way to soft shapes and forms. Hats, meanwhile, bucked this trend, and were elaborately decorated with very wide brims.

From the 1920s to the 1940s, the hardships and the fears of war opened a new era of prosperity and optimism, and a new clothing trend emerged: the Charleston. This trend showed a more emancipated and self-confident woman. Skirts were shortened and the hem now fell just below the knee, either straight or with narrow or flat pleats. Light, comfortable shirts were adopted for summer weather, as were heavy, short, woolen jackets with sweaters for colder seasons. A distinctive touch of elegance was provided by the inevitable cloche hat, worn in every season. It was athletic practice that caused the abandonment of bulky petticoats and all the trappings that had previously characterized women's costumes. Clothes became simpler, with straighter designs, softer fabrics, shorter skirts and dresses designed primarily to allow the most freedom of movement.

77 Bovril, created in 1870, distinguished its brand by using a golfer in its advertising.

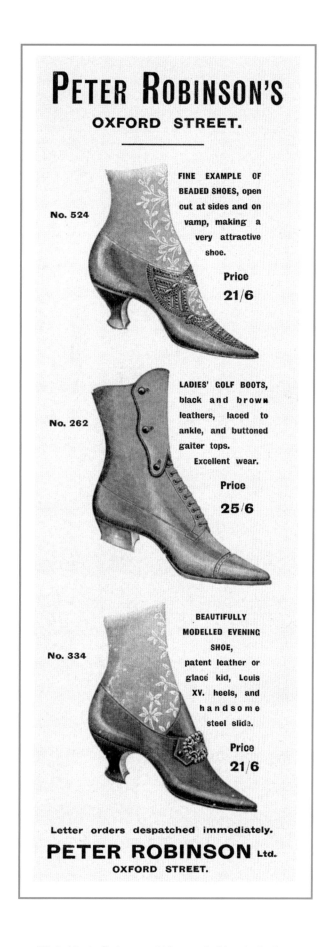

PETER ROBINSON'S
OXFORD STREET.

No. 524

FINE EXAMPLE OF BEADED SHOES, open cut at sides and on vamp, making a very attractive shoe.

Price
21/6

No. 262

LADIES' GOLF BOOTS, black and brown leathers, laced to ankle, and buttoned gaiter tops.
Excellent wear.

Price
25/6

No. 334

BEAUTIFULLY MODELLED EVENING SHOE, patent leather or glacé kid, Louis XV. heels, and handsome steel slide.

Price
21/6

Letter orders despatched immediately.

PETER ROBINSON Ltd.
OXFORD STREET.

78 In Monte Carlo, a world-famous holiday destination, golf was introduced in the early twentieth century at Mont Agel.

79 Elegant golf shoes created by Peter Robinson, a noted Oxford Street shoemaker in 1900.

80 An elegant golfer on the cover of Vogue, the iconic
style magazine founded in 1892.

80-81 In the 1920s, with the arrival of the "Charleston" fashion, skirts got shorter, and legs and arms were on display.

82 Actress Jean Harlow, at the peak of her career,
practicing under the watchful eye of her coach,
Leo Diegel.

83 American film director Howard Hawks (left) explains
a scene to Cary Grant and Katharine Hepburn
on the set of *Bringing Up Baby*.

84 The grace and style of the beautiful Ava Gardner,
pictured in 1942.

85 American champion Betsy Rawls won the Women's
U.S. Open four times.

After the dark years of war, women's fashion regained some of its vigor in the 1950s. Synonymous with the empowerment of women, fashion became more provocative: the modern woman was more daring, and wanted to have fun and to shock. Riding the wave of American fashion, women wore bolder designs, made from lightweight fabrics. Short skirts uncovered the knee and wide and deep necklines became bolder. Miniskirts and shorts appeared, and the bra eventually, and inevitably, disappeared.

Fabrics with strong contrasting colors and simple designs predominated, and in time, led to the establishment of specific collections for the course. These fashions were launched by professionals and followed by golfers on every continent.

During the twentieth century, golfers understood that wearing socks outside the pants was like wearing underwear outside their pants. Common sense prevailed and men began to wear long pants, offsetting their more sober clothing with a bit of color. Since 1970, golfers have experimented with every imaginable color, with designers indulging in combinations that have often been jarring.

Like Jimmy Demaret before him, Doug Sanders devoted time and money to enrich his wardrobe, which consisted of bright colored pants and shirts that always attracted the attention of fans, teammates and opponents. In tournaments, everyone wanted to see what Doug Sanders would wear, though he was also striking in other ways. He had an unusual swing, one of the shortest backswings ever seen on the Tour. While playing, he was often followed by large crowds, among which were many celebrities, like Frank Sinatra, Dean Martin and Evel Knievel. And, as Chi Chi Rodriguez said, Sanders was the best money player he'd ever seen. "A better golfer playing with his money than playing with other people's money."

87 Whimsical golfer Jimmy Demaret opens his colorful wardrobe for photographers. His clothing always distinguished him from his fellow professionals.

Towards the end of the twentieth century, golfers began to dampen their imaginations, focusing on the use of primary colors. The entry of companies like Nike into the golf market facilitated this trend, with the introduction of well-cut polo shirts and baseball caps. In the new millennium, fashion has stabilized, although some people have struck out in their choice of clothing.

The rookie Rickie Fowler usually chooses monochromatic clothing, especially on Sundays when he favors a bright orange. Japan's Ryo Ishikawa focuses on pastel colors, while Tiger Woods uses a red T-shirt on the final day of competition. Black, however, has always been appreciated as a slimming, sexy and intimidating color. Gary Player is the godfather of this color, even if he showed up at the Masters wearing white pants with one white leg and one black leg.

Who has the best fashion sense in golf and who has the worst? Ian Poulter could be ranked in the top rank in a poll on the most unusual and striking clothing, although the Englishman has moderated his stylistic choices over the years. In 2005, in anticipation of the Open Championship at St. Andrews, Poulter had the temerity to hold a competition among young designers in Britain. The result was a pair of bizarrely styled pants that featured the Claret Jug on his right leg and a list of past Open winners on the back of the left leg. Poulter was the first player from the 1990s to introduce irony in clothing, and his unique, eye-catching hairstyles were soon imitated by young fans.

Today, numerous other players are distinguished by unconventional styles, from the t-shirts designed by Duffy Waldorf and the pants of John Daly to the polo shirts of Jim Furyk.

Women, meanwhile, have begun to wear nimble, elegant, and colorful clothes, led by Natalie Gulbis, Maria Verchenova, Paula Creamer, Diana Luna and many other followers of Laura Baugh, the Californian who, in the early 1970s, sparked the imagination of many fans. Voted the most beautiful and elegant golfer in 1971, she would become the richest golfer in the world at the time, with numerous endorsements and sponsors.

88 Beautiful and talented Laura Baugh won the title of "Woman of the Year" and "The Most Beautiful Golfer of all Time."

90 American rising star Rickie Fowler is distinguished
not only for his play, but also his colorful clothing, though
he always wears orange in the final round.

91 Japan's Ryo Ishikawa, a great player from a young
age, has always sported a lively fashion sense.

I REGARD GOLF AS AN EXPENSIVE WAY OF PLAYING MARBLES.

G.K. Chesterton

92 AND 93 Tiger Woods isn't the only golfer to have club head covers depicting a tiger. Ryo Ishikawa actually uses his caricature as a cover for his driver and as a distinctive mark on the ball. Often, there is a great demand from fans for these club head covers.

94 Early in his career, Payne Stewart decided how to stand out from other professionals, wearing his colorful "plus fours."

95 South African champion Gary Player was dubbed the "Black Knight" for his color preference.

96 AND 96-97 Eccentric almost to the point of madness, controversial American champion John Daly, winner of two Major titles, launched a very successful line of clothing and accessories.

98 American Paula Creamer, one of the more attractive women on the American Tour, stood out by always wearing a pink item of clothing.

99 Russian beauty Maria Verchenova can afford to play with extremely feminine flouncy skirts that accentuate her legs.

100-101 Players often have questionable taste, as in the case of Sakura Yokomine, here in a dispute with the Women's U.S. Open.

GOLF IS LIFE. IF YOU
DO NOT LIKE GOLF,
YOU CAN NOT APPRE-
CIATE LIFE.
Anonymous

101 Recently, shorts, worn here by Jennifer Rosales,
have come into fashion among women golfers.

102 AND 103 Women on the Tour never lack femininity. Attentive to every detail, from clothes to accessories, they don't forget to always add a personal touch, even to the bag and club head covers, which are often good luck charms.

The Fascination with Golf's Classic Tournaments

The Grand Slam, the top prize in golf, is the only sought-after title that does not offer a cup, a trophy or cash as a prize. Not assigned by any authority or committee, this "invisible" honor has been up for grabs since 1931, but no player has ever won it. There may not be a prize as such but professional golfers would do almost anything to win the Grand Slam, which requires the winning of all four of the Major titles — the Open, the U.S. Open, the PGA and the Masters — in the same year.

104 Bobby Jones (left) with the four Grand Slam trophies he won in 1930: the U.S. and British Amateurs, the Open Championship and U.S. Open.

105 Bobby Jones in action at Augusta.

The Masters Tournament

This idea was originally put forward by a journalist who did not actually play golf, but wrote with unsurpassed expertise. His inspiration for the Grand Slam was a series of victories in 1930 that have not been repeated since. That year, a young amateur American, Robert Tyre Jones Jr., better known as Bobby Jones, won the Open, the U.S. Open along with the American and British Amateur Championships.

Jones, however, did not come from the golf world. He was, in fact, a lawyer and an engineer. At 28, married with young children to provide for, he was charged with taking care of his family's affairs. His family was, at the time, one of the most well-known, respected and wealthy families in Georgia. After leaving the competitive world of golf, he came up with the idea of creating a nice golf course near to where he was raised, and he soon transformed a botanical garden for this purpose. Thus was born the Augusta National. Inviting friends who were professional players, he invented what is now called the Masters Tournament — one of the four Majors of the Grand Slam. Today, a winning streak like Jones' would be almost impossible to achieve: no amateur in the world would be able to win all four events. The only amateur to bring home a second place at the U.S. Open was Jack Nicklaus in 1960 (he was beaten by Arnold Palmer). Bobby Jones' quadruple victory in 1930 captivated America, and the public was hungry for a way to share the many facets of golf. A journalist named Oscar Baun Keeler, picky, precise and informed, had a close association with Jones, and his articles soon became the most reliable source for all those who wanted to know something about the amateur golfer.

Since 1930, nobody has been able to repeat Jones' feats. Yet we continue to talk about the Grand Slam, the title everyone wants to snatch. Some thought Tiger Woods would be the one to achieve it, dominating the sport the way he did at the turn of 2000. But it didn't happen. Like Tiger Woods, many champions have won all four Grand Slam events, but unfortunately, in different years. Nicklaus was the best of all, with six Masters, four U.S. Opens, three Opens and five PGA championships, totaling eighteen victories. Behind him is Tiger Woods with fourteen titles, then Walter Hagen with eleven and Ben Hogan with nine, including three in 1953.

107 The opening shot of the 1936 Masters by Bobby Jones, the champion who created a tournament to meet up with his friends once a year.

108-109 A tee shot on the 12th hole, the second hole of the Amen Corner at Augusta, a trio of hellish holes from the 11th to 13th.

109 TOP Jack Nicklaus and Arnold Palmer, Honorary Starters at the 2010 Masters. Traditionally, a former winner inaugurates the tournament with the first drive.

109 CENTER Ian Poulter is disconsolate after a missed putt on the 13th hole. It is not uncommon to see reactions like these on the notoriously terrible greens at Augusta.

109 BOTTOM Australian champion Adam Scott has never won a Major, despite the high hopes many have had for him.

110-111 K.J. Choi putts on the treacherous sloping green at the 9th hole. In the background, you can see spectators, and the buildings that make up the club house.

111 A view of the scenic, par 3, 16th hole, which features a lake between the tee and the green and a natural platform on the left that holds thousands of spectators.

112 TOP One of the most unusual and colorful characters of the American Tour: Colombian Camilo Villegas studying the line of a putt.

112 BOTTOM 16-year old Italian Matteo Manassero was the youngest participant in the 2010 Masters and the youngest amateur to make the cut.

112-113 Tiger in action: Tiger Woods, winner of 14 Majors, including four Masters: 1997, 2001, 2002 and 2005.

114 A shot of the awards ritual during the 2011 Masters prize-giving day.
The winner of the previous edition, Mickelson, is shown here as he helps Schwartzel, the new champion, put on the Green Jacket.

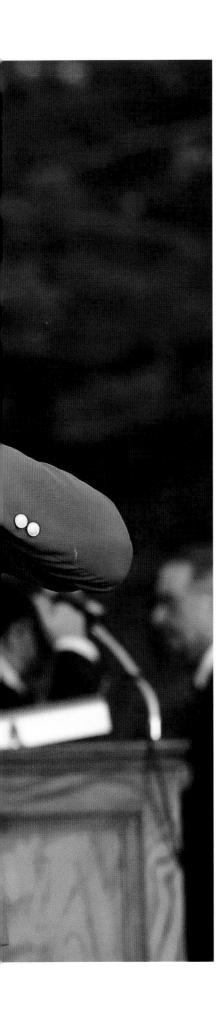

115 South African Charles Schwartzel, during the second
round of the Augusta Masters, April 8, 2011.

US Open

We have already mentioned the Masters, but we must stress the importance of the other three majors. Each one has something that makes it special, unique and incomparable, though arguments and discussions about which is the best are endless. Those who live in the southern United States like the Masters for its location, tradition, ambience and exclusivity. In other areas of the country, the U.S. Open is considered the best tournament to win as it is truly open to all, and represents a dream for most American golfers. It is, for many, the American tournament par excellence, a party and celebration that almost rivals the atmosphere and fandom of the Ryder Cup. The courses where the Ryder Cup is played are rarely the same, and its location has varied since the first edition in 1895, won by Englishman Horace Rawlins. After an initial British monopoly of the tournament, it was dominated almost entirely by Americans or, rather, the players who usually play on the PGA Tour.

Europeans, until 2010, have traditionally not been among the top rankings. For them the U.S. Open had, seemingly, been cursed until 1971, when Englishman Tony Jacklin won it. The admission rules did not allow many Europeans to participate and, moreover, the pre-qualification was very difficult. Just consider the fact that there were more than 9000 players (2010 was a record year with 9457 entrants) and they started two months previously, on more than 90 courses. Historically, the U.S. Open is played on courses that verge on the brutal, as the USGA, the organizer, wants the winner to be truly the best there is. The fairways, therefore, do not exceed 85 ft (26 m) wide, the first cut of rough reaches 4 in (10 cm) and the second nearly 14 in (36 cm) while those around the greens are cut to 3 in (8 cm). Although the undulations of the greens change often, the speeds measured by the Stimpmeter (the instrument that measures the speed of the putting green) range from 6.5 to 10.5 ft (2.0 to 3.2 m).

116 Englishman Tony Jacklin was the previous European to win the U.S. Open, in 1970, before Graeme McDowell brought the title back to Europe in 2010.

118-119 Tiger in action at Oakmont. Woods has three victories at the U.S. Open, the latest being the dramatic 2008 win at Torrey Pines.

YOU SELDOM LOSE A BOWLING BALL. Anonymous

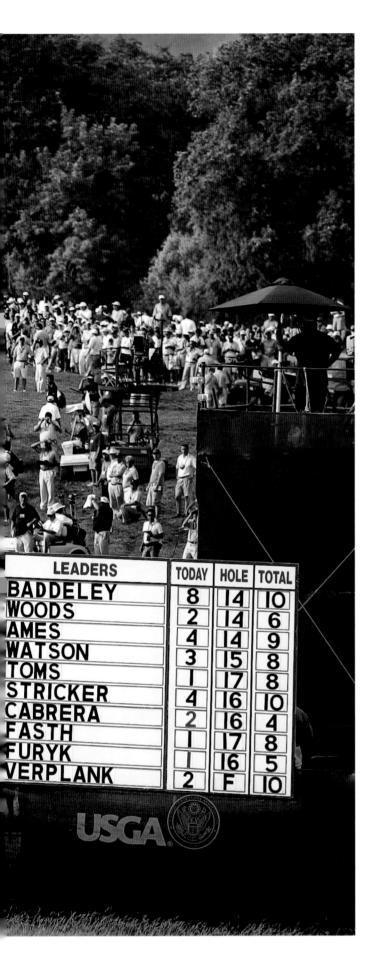

LEADERS	TODAY	HOLE	TOTAL
BADDELEY	8	14	10
WOODS	2	14	6
AMES	4	14	9
WATSON	3	15	8
TOMS	1	17	8
STRICKER	4	16	10
CABRERA	2	16	4
FASTH	1	17	8
FURYK	1	16	5
VERPLANK	2	F	10

USGA.®

119 The clubhouse at Oakmont Country Club, the American course
that has hosted the largest number of Majors.

120-121 Ernie Els putting on the 9th green at Torrey Pines under the watchful eye of Geoff Ogilvy.

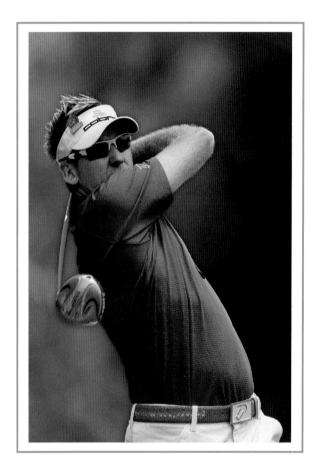

121 Englishman Ian Poulter is one of the most
accomplished players at the moment, and a strong
candidate to win a Major.

122-123 Courses that host the U.S. Open are deliberately made more difficult. This is a glimpse of Bethpage Black, where it was last played in 2009.

123 TOP At Bethpage Black, Tiger Woods finds his ball,
with the help of a judge, in the thick rough
on the edge of a bunker.

123 BOTTOM Adam Scott gets out of a bunker during
the 109th edition of the U.S. Open played
at Bethpage Black, New York.

IF YOU THINK IT'S HARD TO MEET NEW PEOPLE, TRY PICKING
UP THE WRONG GOLF BALL.

Jack Lemmon

124 The world's most famous left-hander, Phil Mickelson,
holds the record for most second-place finishes in U.S.
Open history with five : 1999, 2002, 2004, 2006 and 2009.

125 Lucas Glover kisses the U.S. Open trophy at
Bethpage Black in 2009.

126 The 7th green at Pebble Beach, California overlooking the Pacific Ocean.
This is one of the most famous holes in the world. Nicklaus himself was
involved in its redesign.

126-127 The bunkers at Pebble Beach pose a lot of problems due to the tufts of wild grass that swallow balls hit out of bounds.

128 Experience in the Majors is very important and Ryo
Ishikawa, although very young, already has plenty.
The Japanese champion hit the headlines in 2008,
at just 17 years of age.

129 Surrounded by oceans, the first tee is above
the sea: this is Pebble Beach, which hosted the
tournament, for the fifth time, in 2010.

130 Graeme McDowell, the Irish player who brought the trophy back to Europe, 40 years after the success of Englishman Tony Jacklin.

131 Tiger Woods reacts to having missed a birdie during the 2010 U.S. Open at Pebble Beach.

PGA Championship

The PGA Championship, meanwhile, has always been considered the Cinderella of the Majors, but in recent years it has increased in importance, and is now coveted by players. Organized by the PGA of America (which oversees all tournaments throughout the year), it is here that the association expresses all of its power and excellence in game development and assistance to its members, following the principles of its founder: Rodman Wanamaker. When Wanamaker inherited a chain of department stores from his father, he revolutionized the concept of what those stores could be, focusing on fine furnishings and eye-catching displays to promote sales. A versatile man who was ahead of his time, Wanamaker dabbled in numerous fields, introducing cashiers in his supermarkets, buying the largest aircraft ever built at that time (for the first flight across the Atlantic to France), and staging the first show for fans at a major sporting event. This frenetic pace continued until he discovered golf. Radically changing his habits, he devoted himself entirely to the development of the game and the birth of the Professional Golfers' Association of America. As a promotional stunt, he met Walter Hagen and many other great players of the time, such as Francis Ouimet and A.W. Tillinghast, on 17 January 1916, at the Taplow Club in New York City. The aim of the meeting was to give life to a great professional association. In two months, he found 82 supporters, and on 10 April 1916, the association of American professionals was born, in a hotel in New York.

Among the first activities initiated by Wanamaker was the creation of a championship in which American champions could compete against British champions at match play. In mid-October 1916, the PGA Championship was born. The Championship would stay with the match play format until 1958, after which it switched to its current 72-hole stroke play format.

133 The PGA Championship trophy, which takes its name from its donor, Rodman Wanamaker, the founder, in 1916, of the Professional Golfers' Association of America.

ANNUAL
CHAMPIONSHIP
OF THE
PROFESSIONAL
GOLFERS
ASSOCIATION
AMERICA
TROPHY

134 Medinah is one of the preferred locations for major tournaments. It hosted the 2006 PGA Championship, and will host the 2012 Ryder Cup.

134-135 Steve Stricker approaches the 9th green at the Winged Foot Golf Club, where the Major was played in 2006.

136-137 Irishman Padraig Harrington won his third Major title, the 2008 PGA Championship at Oakland Hills.

137 Camilo Villegas plays a tee shot at the 6th hole at Oakland Hills in 2006.

138-139 Swede Henrik Stenson plays from a fairway bunker during the final stage of the 91st PGA Championship at the Hazeltine National Golf Club in Chaska in 2009.

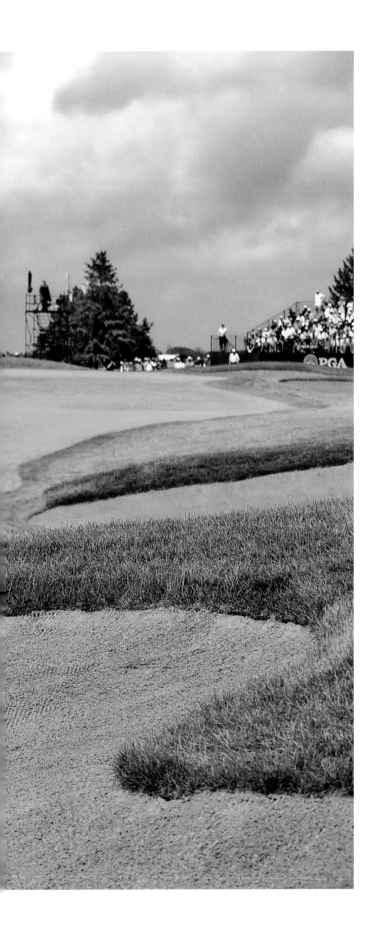

139 Y.E. Yang's win in 2009 was a surprise. Many had predicted a Tiger Woods victory.

140 In just three years, Martin Kaymer has progressed from the European Challenge
Tour to win the 2010 PGA Championship at Whistling Straits.

140-141 Martin Kaymer is the second German player to win a Major after the great Bernhard Langer, who won at Augusta.

142-143 AND 143 Martin Kaymer on the 17th hole at Whistling Straits in Wisconsin, on the shores of Lake Michigan.

The holes by the lake are always exposed to strong winds, which greatly complicates play.

Open Championship

Across the Atlantic, in Britain, it was believed that the Claret Jug, the Open Championship trophy, was still the real prize in golf. It was, by then, 150 years old (but it did not look its age). With 11 interruptions caused by wars, this is the oldest major tournament in the world and brings with it tradition and charisma that cannot be found anywhere else. To keep this tradition intact, the Royal & Ancient Golf Club of St. Andrews always organizes the tournament on the same courses, although they rotate hosting duties. One of the oldest is Muirfield, home of the organization that invented the tournament in 1860. The Honourable Company of Edinburgh Golfers had hosted the Open Championship six times on the public nine-hole course at Musselburgh before deciding to build the private course of Muirfield, which hosted the Open for the first time in 1892. In fact, the tournament was played only nine months after completing work on the course. This was the first of 15 times the tournament would be played there. An English amateur, Harold Hilton, won with a score of 78-81-74-72 in front of an audience estimated at 100 people. Hilton played in secret: his father did not want him to participate and the young amateur traveled all night, by train, to appear on the tee of the first hole without even having taken any practice swings. Four years later, the great Harry Vardon won the first of his six wins (which remains unbeaten record) while still a teenager. Following criticism after the first edition, the course was lengthened by more than 1600 ft (488 m). Vardon won after a long, 36-hole, play-off with John Henry Taylor. The competition left Prestwick in 1873, with St. Andrews becoming the custodian.

145 An old poster, from the beginning of the twentieth century, promoting golf and The Open Championship.

At the heart of the tournament, however, is the Claret Jug, the trophy is steeped in history and engraved with the names of the greatest champions that ever trod the fairways. This cup, which is the oldest trophy in the world (even tennis, cricket and sailing do not have cups as old as that), never actually leaves the glass case at the entrance of the headquarters of the Royal & Ancient Golf Club of St. Andrews. A smaller replica, in fact, is delivered to the winner. The immense value of the cup's history prevents it from the leaving the heavily protected R-&-A premises, with even the televised engraving of the latest winner done on the replica.

The origins of the Open Championship began with the death of Allan Robertson, a professional and the greenskeeper at St. Andrews. At the time, he was considered the top player in the world. Following his death, in 1859, many felt the need to establish a tournament that to honor his memory and help determine who would become his successor. So, in 1860, a tournament was held in Prestwick, with players competing for a leather belt with a bronze plaque. Old Tom Morris was also active at that time, and was friendly with Robertson both on and off the fairway. In fact, the two produced golf equipment together until they had an argument, in 1848, when Old Tom used gutta-percha to cover the balls and insisted on spreading its use and production. Robertson, who ran the business side of the company, was tied to the feathery balls and opposed the decision, supporting their use in tournaments long after other players of the time.

Tom Morris won the Open Championship in three consecutive years, from 1868 to 1870, and was, finally, and definitively, awarded the belt. In 1871 the tournament was not played as it was seeking funds for a new trophy, the Claret Jug. Among the interesting facts about the trophy: only three amateurs (Bobby Jones, Harold Hilton and John Ball) have ever won it, and Harry Vardon has won it the most times. The Open Championship, "the Open," or "the British Open" to the uninitiated, always charms fans with its old-world magic, but it still manages to stay relevant. It was, in fact, best described by Tiger Woods, who said, "It is about more than sport, a mid-summer party." Americans such as Sam Snead, have tried to snub it. He once returned from St. Andrews and said that he had played on a field of turnips. But, in the end, all great champions have understood the fascination and frustration of playing the Open. Walter Hagen went there. As did Arnold Palmer and Jack Nicklaus. And now, Tiger has come back. Local spectators are aware of this and proud: they want to see the very best champions "in contention." From Arnie's plate (on what is now the 16th hole at Royal Birkdale) to the photographs of Gary Player on the wall at Royal Lytham & St. Annes, the Open is many things: history, tradition, the rain from the sea and the breeze in your face. It is a ball in flight between broom and grass, the third week of July, a period full of surprises, not all of which are pleasant.

147 Old Tom Morris won four Open Championships. The last time was in 1867.
The following year the title passed to his son, Young Tom Morris.

THE REASON THE PRO TELLS YOU TO KEEP YOUR HEAD DOWN IS SO YOU CAN'T SEE HIM LAUGHING.

Phyllis Diller

148 TOP Stewart Cink in action at Turnberry in the victorious 2009 Open Championship, won against the great Tom Watson.

148 BOTTOM Stewart Cink celebrates a birdie on the 18th hole during the 2009 Open Championship.

149 At Turnberry in 2009, Tom Watson excited fans around the world by coming close to winning, at the age of 59. He was only beaten in a playoff.

150 At St. Andrews, you can breathe golf at every corner of the medieval village, which is the background for every picture. Here, there are always a lot of spectators.

150-151 It is emotional for anyone to hit a drive on the 18th hole of the old course. In the background stands the building of the Royal & Ancient Golf Club of St. Andrews.

152-153 The most famous bunker in the world is on the right side of the 17th green at St. Andrews.

A very deep bunker, it has been the site of many disasters, even for some of the world's strongest players.

153 It is very important in golf to study the lines of putts and the slopes of greens. Here Oliver Wilson studies the 1st green at St. Andrews.

154 AND 155 South African Louis Oosthuizen
conquered St. Andrews in 2010, topping the list from
the second day, and countering the comeback attempts
of numerous big name opponents. For him,
it was the first Major title, for which he won
the legendary Claret Jug.

Ryder Cup

Every Major, therefore, has its own special qualities, its reasons for importance. There is, of course, another major tournament that we must not forget: the Ryder Cup, which, in a sense, is the most British of golf competitions, and certainly one of the most fascinating in the world. It was first played in 1927.

The creation of the Ryder Cup, however, began the year before, a few weeks before the 1926 Open Championship. For that edition, the Royal & Ancient Golf Club of St. Andrews established that all participants had to play a qualifying round. Americans, therefore, had to expect a longer stay in Europe. In those days Atlantic crossings were made by ocean liner and crossings were infrequent. Because of this, American players willingly accepted the idea of forming a team and competing, in an unofficial manner, against a similar English team, at Wentworth. There, among the sparse but knowledgeable audience was a certain Samuel Ryder. Born in 1858, he was the only son of a Manchester corn merchant, and he would soon become very rich, thanks to a brilliantly simple idea. His idea was to market flower seeds, in packets, for a penny each.

The day of the match in Wentworth found him sitting over a cup of tea with two English players, Abe Mitchell and George Duncan. Walter Hagen and Emmett French then arrived and the talk turned to the creation of a regular competition such as the one they had just played. Ryder's interest was piqued. George Duncan suggested to putting up a Cup of some kind as a trophy. Ryder decided that this cup should be gold and that the lid should be topped with a statuette of a golfer. Ryder wanted that statuette to be of Abe Mitchell, the man who had taught him to play the game and had helped to reveal its secrets and joys.

At that time, there was no Order of Merit or money list. So, Ryder resorted to the famous Triumvirate: the composition of the first English team would be decided by Henry Vardon, James Braid and John Henry Taylor, who were widely considered to be the greatest British golfers of the time.

The contest was an instant success and it would continue to grow, increasing the golfing rivalry between Britain and the United States. The scene, of course, would then widen. While American participation in the team was limited to professionals born in the United States, Britain changed the rules of its team, adding four invited players to the eight selected through a points system. Despite this, the American team was increasingly successful, as they had the benefit of selecting players from a much larger pool of talent. Suggestions were soon made to include players from the rest of Europe, and even Jack Nicklaus gave his support to that idea.

The first European players added to the team were Severiano Ballesteros and Ignacio Garrido. Ballesteros and Nick Faldo, would become two of the most important Ryder Cup players. With this new era of players, regulations also underwent changes. Currently, teams are made up of twelve players chosen either on merit or called up by team captains. Teams meet on the morning of the first day in 4 foursome matches, and in the afternoon, in 4 fourball matches. The same program is played on the second day. On the third day, all twelve players face each other in match play.

The history of the Ryder Cup is all in a few statistics: in 38 editions (the competition was suspended between 1939 and 1945 for World War II, and postponed for a year in 2001, following the attack on World Trade Center), there have been 26 American wins, 10 European wins (since 1979 the competition has been between a team representing The United States and a team representing the whole of Europe) and two draws. Europe's most sensational victories were those at Oakland Hills in 2004 and the K Club in 2006. The American team's most dominant performance was in 1967, in Houston. Thanks to the enthusiasm of Samuel Ryder, the fans, and most especially the players, who compete for free, the attraction of the Ryder Cup is surely destined to live on.

157 The American team that won the Ryder Cup, in 1931.
At the center, with the cup in his hand, is team captain Walter Hagen.

158 Paul Casey celebrates a hole in one at the 14th hole of the K Club with his foursome partner David Howell during the second day of the tournament.

158-159 The 18th green of the K Club in Ireland, which hosted a triumphant year for the European team in the 2006 Ryder Cup.

160-161 Ian Poulter in action during the 2008 Ryder Cup. The Englishman interpreted the spirit of the event perfectly, with great energy and sportsmanship.

161 A huge crowd watches Padraig Harrington's approach to the 18th green of Valhalla. In Kentucky, there were 40,000 spectators every day.

162-163 Champagne for the Americans who, in 2008, recaptured the Gold Cup after nine years of European domination.

163 U.S. team captain Paul Azinger is swamped
by his players after their victory at the Valhalla Golf Club
in Kentucky.

164 The attack on the ball of American Dustin Johnson, on a drive from the 5th hole at Celtic Manor, which hosted the 2010 Ryder Cup.

164-165 The spectators at the Ryder Cup often play a leading role in the proceedings, not only because of their large numbers, but also because of the often colorful and fun clothing worn, as seen on the 17th tee at Celtic Manor.

166 A celebratory gesture after Lee Westwood sinks a putt for a birdie on the 5th hole at Celtic Manor in 2010.

167 Lee Westwood from Britain, observes the trajectory of his shot, during the Ryder Cup of 2010.

The Fascination with Golf's Classic Tournaments

Golf has changed over the centuries and has also changed the face of female athletics, providing a long line of champions capable of attracting crowds and stealing sports coverage from their male colleagues. Joyce Wethered, winner of the first Women's British Open Amateur Championship, counted Bobby Jones and Gene Sarazen as loyal fans, while Babe Zaharias was winning Olympic medals and world athletics then devoting herself to golf at the age of 23. Women's golf saw other major champions like Nancy Lopez, Mickey Wright, Kathy Whitworth, and Catherine Lacoste before the arrival of the extraordinary Annika Sorenstam, Lorena Ochoa, Karrie Webb and a platoon of Asian players who imposed themselves on the golf world with countless victories. Since 2007, the Women's British Open has been played at St. Andrews, putting women's golf on a par with the men's game.

Even the ladies, then, have their Majors and the chance to win the Grand Slam. Like the men, however, that, until now, remains to be achieved. Also like men's golf, three of the Majors are played in the U.S. and one in the U.K. The LPGA Championship is similar to the PGA Championship and the Kraft Nabisco Championship is equivalent to the Masters. In the latter case, there are many similarities: both are the first Majors of their respective season, both are held on the same course every year, and both have a unique tradition for the winner: the green jacket at the Masters and the "jump in the lake on the 18th hole" at the Kraft Nabisco.

The Majors in women's golf (with the exception of the Women's U.S. Open) also have a sponsor included in tournament names (or, in the case of the LPGA Championship, a sponsor whose name appears after the name of the tournament). Moreover, the LPGA organizes two of its four Majors, namely the Kraft Nabisco and the LPGA Championship. The Women's U.S. Open, like its male equivalent, is managed by the United States Golf Association. The Women's British Open is run by the Ladies' Golf Union, the governing body of women's golf in the United Kingdom and Ireland. And, after nearly 70 years of men's Ryder Cup history, professional women players were finally given their own version of the tournament in 1990: the Solheim Cup.

169 A young Glenna Collett Vare was a finalist in the 1929 British Ladies Amateur Championship, where she lost 1-3 to champion Joyce Wethered.

Women's British Open

170-171 Mexican champion Lorena Ochoa gets out of the bunker at the 18th hole at Royal Lytham & St. Annes in 2006.

171 Disappointment mixed with anger can be seen on the face of Ai Miyazato after a missed putt in the Women's British Open at Royal Lytham & St. Annes.

172 TOP South African Ashleigh Simon crosses the
Swilcan Bridge, the bridge over the stream at the 18th
hole of the Old Course at St. Andrews, in 2007.

172 BOTTOM The 17th hole at St. Andrews is also
known as "the Road Hole," with a terrible bunker, which
the Korean In-Bee Park can be seen getting out of.

172-173 A drive from the 18th tee at St. Andrews by the beautiful Natalie Gulbis, one of the stars of the 2007 tournament won by Lorena Ochoa.

174-175 Japan's Mika Miyazato gets out of the bunker during the Ricoh's 2009 Women's British Open played at Royal Lytham & St Annes.

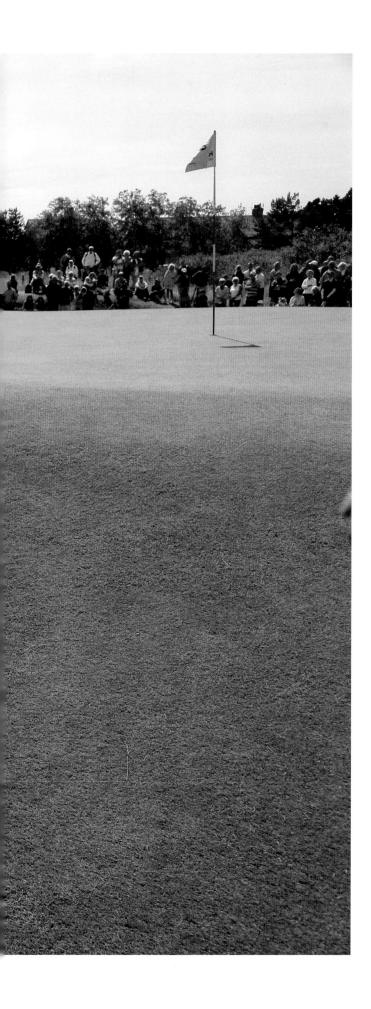

175 The "Pink Panther" Paula Creamer attacks the ball during Ricoh's 2009 Women's British Open.

176 AND 177 Body language often expresses more than
words. The outgoing and exuberant Christina Kim (left)
and the reserved and controlled Marianne Skarpnord
react to missed putts during the Women's British Open.

178-179 Yani Tseng's approach to the 18th at Royal Birkdale, where she won with a one stroke advantage.

WHEN I DIE, BURY ME ON
THE GOLF COURSE SO MY
HUSBAND WILL VISIT.

Anonymous

179 Ai Miyazato plays the second shot on the 1st hole,
into the wind, during the 2010 Women's British Open at
Royal Birkdale.

180-181 Yani Tseng in 2010 gave Taiwan its first title in a Major and is congratulated by Christina Kim.

181 In-Kyung Kim after missing her putt during the
Women's British Open at Royal Birkdale.

LPGA Championship

182-183 After winning the Major, Anna Nordqvist, as is the tradition, kisses the trophy she has just won.

183 Sweden's Anna Nordqvist hits it on the green at the 4th hole during the second round of McDonald's 2009 LPGA Championship.

Kraft Nabisco Championship

184-185 Suzann Pettersen hits a drive on the 18th hole on the Dinah Shore course at the Mission Hills Country Club, home of the Kraft Nabisco Championship.

185 The "Nabisco" is the first Major of the season and has always been played on the same course. Karen Stupples plays a tee shot on the 18th hole.

U.S. Women's Open

186 A drive by Michelle Wie, during the 2006 U.S.
Women's Open Golf Championship. Wie has never won
a Major, causing some to feel she has been overrated.

187 Sweden's Annika Sorenstam, retired at the peak of
her career, having won the U.S. Women's.
Open three times.

A PASSION, AN OBSESSION, A ROMANCE,
A NICE ACQUAINTANCESHIP WITH TREES,
SAND, AND WATER.

Bob Ryan

188 Italy's Giulia Sergas gets out of a bunker during the 2008 U.S. Women's
Open played at Interlachen.

188-189 Despite a glittering career, and a world number one ranking, Lorena Ochoa has never managed to win this Major.

190-191 Natalie Gulbis gets out of the bunker during the first round of the 2010 U.S. Women's. Open at the Oakmont Country Club.

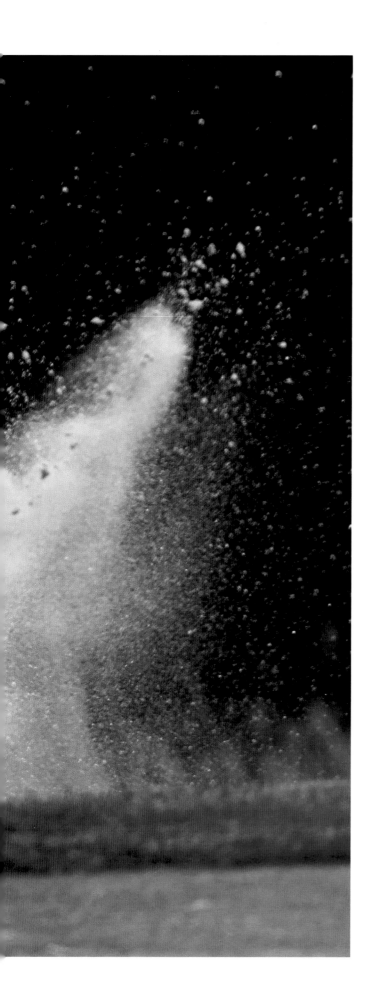

191 The "Pink Panther," Paula Creamer, at the start of the 2010 U.S. Women's Open. Her first Major win, she beat Suzann Pettersen and Na Yeon Choi.

Solheim Cup

192-193 Paula Creamer, star of the U.S. team, gets out of the bunker on the 8th hole during a match played in Halmstad, Sweden, in 2007.

193 Veteran Juli Inkster hits a tee shot during the successful
tournament held in Sweden.

194 Tania Elosegui in action during the 2009 Solheim Cup played in Sugar Grove, Illinois.

GOLF IS ESSENTIALLY AN
EXERCISE IN MASOCHISM
CONDUCTED OUT OF DOORS.
Paul O'Neil

195 Janice Moodie of the European team wearing
shorts in the final round at Sugar Grove.

196 The very young Hawaiian Michelle Wie also wearing shorts during match play in 2009.

196-197 The unity of the team is often seen in the fine detail. Paula Creamer did not skimp on glasses, ball markers and U.S. flags.

198 Morgan Pressel, who secured the winning point at
the 2009 Solheim Cup, is congratulated by teammates,
with Juli Inkster leading the charge.

199 Christina Kim and Michelle Wie celebrate on the
second day of the 2009 Solheim Cup.

The Fascination with Golf's Magnificent Courses

*I*t's not easy choosing the most beautiful golf courses in the world: some are rewarding in a sporting sense and others are more pleasing to the eye. Some people prefer difficult courses, whereas others, like "the Sunday golfer" are happy just to imagine themselves alongside the pros. Of course, there are also those who just enjoy the beautiful scenery, seeing golf as a relaxed walk that lets them take in the greenery, the lakes, the sea and the mountains.

One thing everyone loves, however, is playing on famous courses where history has been made. Who would not want to see the places where events occurred that have filled golf's history books? Those courses have become famous for their challenges and technical characteristics, which have allowed them to become part of the modern day international circuit of tournaments. Of course, some are included for other reasons, like the "historic" St. Andrews or Carnoustie, to name but two.

We need to remember that golf is one of the few sports that does not have a standardized playing field: each course is unique even if some elements are common to all. A regulation course is composed of 18 holes, each with its own tee at distances that vary between 100 yds (92 m) and 600 yds (550 m) from the hole. From the tee to the hole runs a fairway flanked on either side by high, uncut grass (the rough). There may also be various types of obstacles to make it harder to reach the hole: trees, sand bunkers, and ponds or lakes. To be easily identifiable from a distance, the hole is marked by a flag and surrounded by an extensive area of smooth, low cut grass (the green). Every hole is assigned a number of strokes, which the hole should be completed in (par). This number depends on the length of the hole (the distance from the start to the hole). Depending on the value, holes are referred to as "par 3" (98 to 220 yds [90 to 200 m]), "par 4" (230 to 460 yds [210 to 420 m]) or "par 5" (460 to 600 yds [420 to 550 m]). The sum of the different pars on each hole represents the par for the whole course: 18-hole courses can typically vary from par 68 to par 73, but the most common is par 72.

Professional tournaments usually involve four rounds, which total 72 holes. After two rounds competitors are eliminated (the cut). The winner is the player with the lowest score. In the case of a tie, a play-off will be played until there is a winner.

201 Aerial view of Cape Kidnappers, New Zealand, with holes overlooking the ocean.

202-203 The 18th hole with the clubhouse in the background. In an aerial view you can see the winding path of the Barry Burn, the water hazard that runs through the 17th and 18th holes.

203 An aerial view of Carnoustie.

Carnoustie Golf Links

The Royal Burgh of Carnoustie is a village in the county of Angus, on the east coast of Scotland, which owes its fame to the game of golf. The town was founded on the basis of the wonderful links outlined by Allan Robertson and remodeled in 1926 by James Braid, a five-time Open champion. The compact, sandy, soil make it the perfect golf course, to the point that many consider it the most suitable area in the world for a Major. In addition to the design of the holes and the very deep bunkers, the weather conditions, in particular the strong winds, often affect results. During the twentieth and early twenty-first century, the Open Championship was played at Carnoustie seven times (1931, 1937, 1953, 1968, 1975, 1999 and 2007). The course, one of the ten oldest in the world, was created in 1842 with only 10 holes and increased to 18 holes by Old Tom Morris in 1861. The course has been rejuvenated in the last 30 years, mainly to meet modern standards.

204 TOP The 17th green, the "Island," with the three
treacherous bunkers that protect it.

204 BOTTOM Paul Broadhurst playing from the edge of
the Barry Burn that crosses the 18th.

The Austrian Markus Brier gets out of the bunker on the 18th. Bunkers often represent the biggest challenges on a course.

206-207 A picturesque view of the 1st and 18th holes of the Old Course, with the Swilcan Bridge in view.

207 In this image, from the ground, the 8th hole, par 3, is in the foreground, while the 9th hole is in the background.

St. Andrews Old Course

𝒯he Old Course at St. Andrews in Scotland is worthy of a separate mention. This is the "Home of Golf," where the game was played 600 years ago, and the place where the idea of a golf course was developed. Here traditions of the game were born and are still maintained. Despite the presence of six other courses, the best known is the Old Course, whose first tee is right outside the headquarters of the Royal & Ancient Golf Club of St. Andrews, the body that governs world golf. This was the first course built in the village location, just a few miles from Edinburgh, with 22 holes (reduced to 18 in 1764). At the Old Course, seven holes have the same huge greens, with white flags for the front nine and red for the back nine. The course owes its fame to the terrain and the presence of 112 bunkers. Among the symbols of the course are the Swilcan Bridge over the Swilcan Burn, the stream that crosses the fairway at the 1st and 18th holes. From Old Tom Morris and Willie Park, to Jack Nicklaus and Tiger Woods, Swilcan Bridge has represented the defining moment for the winner of every Open Championship at St. Andrews.

208 The green of the 5th hole is protected by the "Hell Bunker."

208-209 In this spectacular aerial view, we can really appreciate the 17th green, known as the "Road Hole."

210-211 The Kingsbarn clubhouse outfitted in typical Scottish style.

211 The priceless panorama enjoyed on the 17th hole, with a stormy sea served as a side dish.

Kingsbarns
Golf Links

*T*owards the end of the eighteenth century, merchants and notables from Kingsbarns came together to found the Kingsbarns Golf Society, where conviviality reigned supreme. They continued to play, eat and drink for decades until Lady Erskine of Cambo, in 1922, inspired the creation of the Kingsbarns Golf Club. Willie Auchterlonie was asked to design a nine-hole course with views over Kingsbarns Bay. Kingsbarns, rejuvenated and recently popular after years of neglect, was already a must-play for those who travel to Scotland for golf. In fact, the course and the clubhouse are so scenic that it's worth exploring simply for the views. Kingsbarns has been redesigned by the American Kyle Phillips, with the help of owner Mark Parsinen, and they have been able to exploit the nature of the terrain and integrate it with the surrounding landscape. The result is breathtaking, a design that embraces the sea at every hole, and leaves most visitors awestruck.

212 The greens at Kingsbarn are often windswept by the sea: the 12th green (top, viewed from the tee) and the 17th green (bottom).

212-213 A bunker, in the foreground, and a mound shape the layout of the 6th hole.

Loch Lomond
Golf Club

*L*och Lomond is a true garden, designed by renowned architect Doug Carrick, with magnificently maintained greens and velvety fairways. Loch Lomond, however, is an exclusive, private, club for 800 lucky members. The 18-hole, 7180 yd (6575 m), par 72 course winds between ancient forests and the shores of the lake. It was designed by Tom Weiskopf and Jay Morrish, and inaugurated in 1994. The signature hole is certainly the 18th, where the scenery is amplified by the ruins of Rossdhu Castle overlooking the green. With huge and elegant furnishings, the clubhouse has two dining rooms and the warm fabrics with characteristically British furniture. Loch Lomond Golf Club is also known as the home of the Barclays Scottish Open in July, which attracts golf enthusiasts from around the world.

214 AND 214-215 The 7th and 8th holes seen from above, with Rossdhu House, the stately and elegant club house.

216 The 4th green (top) and the trees lining the fairway
of the 13th (bottom).

216-217 The final hole, with the Old Tower, awaits players at the end of the course.

218-219 The Westin Turnberry Resort boasts two 36-hole courses, the Kintyre and the Ailsa.

219 LEFT The classic view of Turnberry: the fairway on the 9th hole, with the white lighthouse, and, in the background, the island of Ailsa Craig.

219 RIGHT The 18th hole at Ailsa, with the club house and hotel in the distance.

Turnberry
Aisla Course

*W*ith the sea on one side, you can see the world's most famous golf course lighthouse: few other locations in the world can evoke emotions like the Ailsa Course at Turnberry in Scotland. It does this through its natural surroundings, its history, its design and the spectacle of the Isle of Ailsa Craig, which dominates and protects the course. Some of the most memorable Open Championships have taken place here, with victories from champions like Tom Watson, Greg Norman and Nick Price. Two of the most memorable: the famous "Duel in the Sun" between Watson and Nicklaus, won by the former, and another incident featuring Watson, when, in 2009, he came close to winning just fifteen days short of his 60th birthday. The course is part of a resort surrounded by the most beautiful Scottish landscape.

220-221 The Old Course and the Cashen Course at Ballybunion, seen from above.

221 Small greens, well-defended and often windswept from the sea, are just some of the challenges at Ballybunion. On the right, the 17th green.

Ballybunion
Golf Club

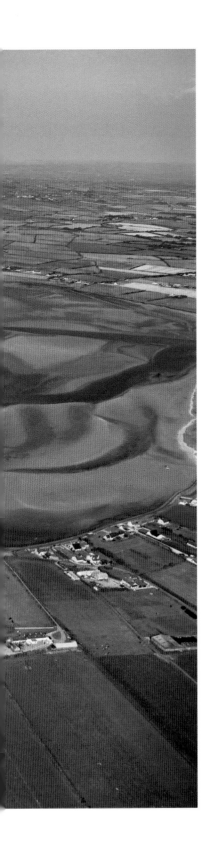

"The island lies like a leaf upon the sea." This is Ireland described by an ancient Celtic poem. On this leaf is placed a precious jewel: the Ballybunion Golf Club. It is the favorite course of the great Tom Watson, who called it the most beautiful and challenging course in the world, and, since 1981, he has never failed to visit it during trips to Ireland. The wind from the sea, the narrow fairways and very deep bunkers have made it difficult to play since 1893, the year of its creation. In 1936 the eccentric British architect Tom Simpson was hired to prepare the ground at the first Irish Amateur Championship, which would be played the following year. Simpson's legacy is formidable, and Ballybunion is a good example, even if Simpson changed very little, implementing what he called "alterations." His gift to posterity lies in the fact that the course's nature has not been "disturbed" or "corrected."

Hamburger Falkenstein Golf Club

𝒴ou can also find several great golf courses near Hamburg in Germany, but the most famous is the Hamburger Falkenstein Golf Club, which dates back to 1930 and is considered to be one of the best in Europe, an absolute masterpiece of design from the brilliant trio of Harry Shapland Colt, John Morrison and Charles Hugh Alison. Hamburger Falkenstein Golf Club is an exceptional course situated in a heathland, amid pine and birch trees with colored areas of heather. With hilly terrain, there are many challenging holes and exciting views. The Hamburger Golf Club was founded in 1906 with a nine-hole course in Flottbek. But with the increased popularity of golf, the course became crowded, and new grounds were finally added to Falkenstein. Most of the original layout remains intact, but the great German designer Bernhard von Limburger made some changes in 1960.

222 AND 222-223 Nature is the star of the show at the Hamburger Falkenstein Golf Club, founded in 1906, but expanded in 1930.

224-225 AND 225 Dense, tall rough, greens that stretch like peninsulas out into the water hazards, huge bunkers that punctuate the immaculate fairways. These are all distinctive trademarks of Robert von Hagge, the Texan architect and the designer of Les Bordes.

Les Bordes

The baron Marcel Bich, an industrialist and creator of the Bic brand of pens, and the businessman Yoshiaki Sokurai thought of designing a new golf course with the goal of creating a place that would attract an international clientele to this corner of the elegant French countryside. To accomplish this, Bich decided to entrust the design of Les Bordes to the Texan Robert von Hagge, a name synonymous with American golf. Soon after its opening, in 1987, Les Bordes was quickly considered to be the second best course in the whole of Europe due to the merits of its creator. Similar in style to courses like the TPC at Sawgrass, Les Bordes is playable from the front tees, while the difficulty from the back tees is extremely high, considering that the course record for professionals, set by Jean Van De Velde, is par. In Les Bordes, accuracy off the tee is essential, in order to avoid the trees and the many lakes.

226-227 The 5th green, seen here during qualifying rounds of the 2010 European Tour.

227 A striking view of the Stadium Course, which is characterized by beautiful landscapes of trees that skirt the fairways.

PGA
de Catalunya

$\mathcal{T}$he PGA Stadium Course in Catalunya, near Barcelona, is a spectacular and imposing location, which, since its opening in 1999, has been consistently ranked among the ten best courses in Europe and has quickly gained an impeccable international reputation. Home to many tournaments on the European Tour, players must play it with great respect, as the beauty of the course can distract you from its many dangers. It makes no concessions with its trees along the sides of the fairways, strategically placed bunkers and lakes that come into play in at least seven of the most difficult holes. The Stadium course is the culmination of over 10 years planning from the designers of the European Tour, who around the end of the 1980s, wanted to build their own course to compete with the U.S. PGA Tour's TPC at Sawgrass. The lush vegetation, the Mediterranean and the abundance of purple heather color each hole. The greens are undulating and always in excellent condition. In addition, there is a number of substantial lakes, which blend perfectly with the landscape, and some holes use water in creative ways.

228 TOP Elliot Saltman playing off one of the few
elevated tees on the Stadium Course.

228 BOTTOM The fairway at the 3rd hole, with the green
in the background.

The Fascination With Golf's Magnificent Courses

228-229 Bunkers and lush foliage are the stars of the PGA in Catalunya. In this image, Englishman Steven Tiley plays a stroke.

Crans-sur-Sierre Golf Club

*I*n Switzerland, you can't miss the Crans sur-Sierre Golf Club, named after the village built around the course. Set in the Valais Alps, on a beautiful plateau overlooking the valley, the course offers splendid panoramic views that have captured the hearts of players like Sergio Garcia and Adam Scott. Several times it has been called the most beautiful mountain-set 18 holes in the world, and it is almost impossible to imagine how, at nearly 5000 ft (1525 m) above sea level, such an impressive course was ever built. The course has a lot of history: from professionals to tourists, the fairways are always crowded in the summer months. The greens have been played by the greatest champions the world: Severiano Ballesteros, who has won the Swiss Open three times there, eventually helped restyle part of the course, which has now been renamed in his honor.

230 LEFT The 18th green, where there is always a crowd of spectators waiting for the final rounds of a competition.

230 RIGHT AND 230-231 The bunkers that surround the 7th green, the hole with the most spectacular view in the world, overlooking the Rhone Valley.

Royal Park
I Roveri

The Royal Park I Roveri was the first Italian course designed by the great Robert Trent Jones Sr., and that alone is a guarantee of quality. Located in the historic Park Herd, hunting area near Turin, the course was built between trees, streams and lakes. The course is technically challenging, with holes designed to force different tactics, and large but undulating greens (characteristic of Trent Jones) representing the greatest challenge. The course dates back to 1971, when it was masterfully integrated with the park which surrounds it. It stands out immediately as the finest Italian golf course for its precise maintenance, the scenery of its holes (each one easily identifiable), its innovative use of bunkers and water hazards, and for its challenging greens and obstacles.

232 AND 232-233 Robert Trent Jones made splendid use of the natural surroundings at Herd Park, a Unesco World Heritage Site.
The Italian Open has been played here on three occasions.

234-235 The water surrounding the Legend Golf Course, owned by the group Constance Hotels Experience.

235 The 18th green with the lake on the right. Every hole at the Legend is unique.

The Legend
Golf Course

*W*hen someone calls himself a legend, there should be constant evidence to back this up. Thankfully, the Legend Golf Course at Belle Mare Plage Resort on the island of Mauritius lives up to its name: everything that has been written and said, since its creation in 1994, is true. A slight breeze always blows, especially in the evening, when you can see deer drinking from the quiet lake around the 18th hole of the course designed by South African champion Hugh Baiocchi. The green on the 18th, like many others on the course, is situated between two lakes, which reflect beautiful, decorative, tropical plants. The area is often frequented by tourists, who find soft fairways interspersed with lakes and surrounded by lush native vegetation.

236 Perfect weather and excellent service allow you to play all year round in absolutely perfect conditions.

236-237 The 17th green, the signature hole of the Legend Course.

238-239 An aerial view shows the picturesque location of the Royal Melbourne Golf Club, overlooking Port Phillip Bay.

239 The 6th hole: an example of Australian designer Alex Russell's work.

Royal Melbourne
Golf Club

$\mathcal{T}$he Royal Melbourne Golf Club, 36 holes designed by Alex Russell, is Australia's oldest and most celebrated course and is generally considered to be the most prestigious and exclusive. It is located just south of the main urban area of Melbourne and was established on 22 May 1891 (it was awarded the title of "Royal" in 1895). The founders were President Sir James McBain and Captain John Munro Bruce (father of the Australian Prime Minister Stanley Melbourne Bruce). Both courses, the East and the West, are considered to be among the best in the world. A combination of holes from the two courses gives us the Composite Course. The current western course was overseen by renowned Australian golfer Alex Russell, who also designed the eastern course, completed in 1932. Both courses are known for their intricate vegetation, the variety of shots required and realistic and exceptionally rapid greens.

240-241 Cliffs overlooking the beautiful Hawkes Bay provide breathtaking scenery at Cape Kidnappers.

241 The 7th hole, a long par 4 (left). The wind sweeps over the 5th green and its deep bunker (right).

Cape Kidnappers
Golf Course

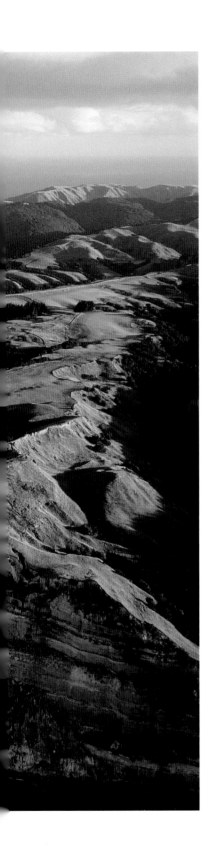

$\mathcal{T}$he Cape Kidnappers course at Hawkes Bay, in New Zealand, is like a lunar landscape. Designed by American architect Tom Doak, it won the 2004 prize for best course in the world thanks to the natural setting in which, in the words of its designer, it was possible to create holes that "do not exist anywhere else in the world." The course is situated overlooks Cape Kidnappers bay, discovered in 1769 by James Cook, the first European to see this part of the island. Cook named it Cape Kidnappers bay after having freed a boy from the hands of a Maori gang which had kidnapped him. The spectacle of the course is unmatched, with holes cut in canyons, dunes and rocky cliffs overlooking the ocean, which, from above, make the holes look like the huge fingers of a prehistoric hand reaching out to the ocean. Exposed to the wind, the holes on the sea are obviously the most difficult and force players to use a more subtle technique.

242-243 The 9th green provides a wonderful view of the Bow River and its surrounding mountains.

243 LEFT The 14th hole, called "Wampum," is a par 4.

243 RIGHT The course seen from above: a strip of green that winds through the Canadian Rockies.

Fairmont Banff Springs Golf Course

$\mathscr{R}$enowned for the scenic beauty of the Canadian Rockies in the heart of the state of Alberta, The Fairmont Banff Springs Golf Course has a captivating and challenging layout. The course offers a breathtaking 360 degree panorama and a difficult to implement design for a high-altitude course, features that highlight the skill of architect Stanley Thompson, who designed it in 1928. The course winds along the Bow River under the snow-capped peaks of Sulphur Mountain and Mount Rundle. In 1989, the course was augmented by the construction of an adjacent nine-hole course designed by Cornish and Robinson, bringing the total to 27 holes. Amateurs and professionals have always been caught up in the emotion of the landscape, thanks to the optical illusions created by the surrounding mountains.

Oakmont Country Club

Oakmont Country Club is the historic club that has hosted the largest number of Majors in the U.S. — seven Open Championships, five Amateur Championships, three PGA Championships and a Women's Open Championship. Few courses in the world have more tradition with Majors, a strange coincidence for a course designed by a building architect, Henry C. Fownes who, in 1903, decided, almost on a whim, to try to build a golf course. The result is there for all to see. This course is, perhaps, the most difficult in all of North America, with 210 very deep bunkers, very difficult greens with terrible slopes and narrow fairways that require pinpoint accuracy. Even today it is said that at Oakmont "the most beautiful round of the twentieth century" was played: the decisive 63 played by Johnny Miller in the final of the 1973 U.S. Open. Located 15 ml (24 km) north-east of Pittsburgh, Oakmont saw Jack Nicklaus get the first of his 18 Majors, in 1962, after a playoff against Arnold Palmer.

244 Englishman Justin Rose gets out of a bunker on the 9th green, in front of the Oakmont clubhouse.

244-245 Even in the absence of trees, the rough and the bunkers can pose great challenges in a course as hard as Oakmont.

246-247 The bunkers always play a role in tournaments at Oakmont.

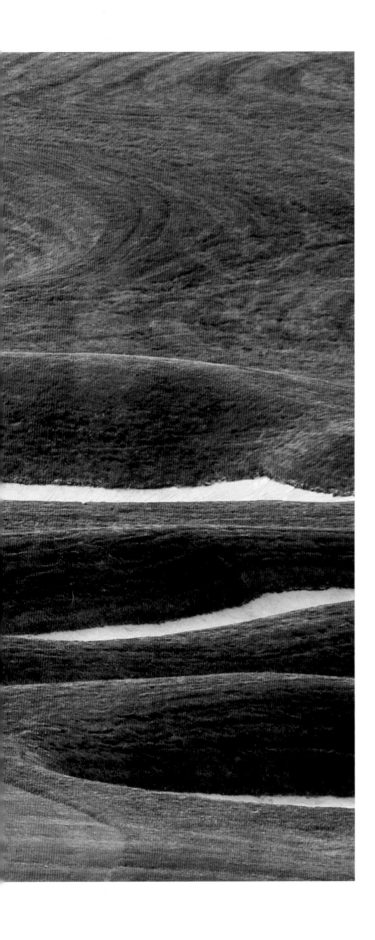

247 Two views of the famous bunker at the 3rd hole, known as the "Church Pew."

Augusta National Golf Club

$\mathcal{A}$ugusta National in Georgia is undoubtedly the most famous course in the world and brings out the glory and history of the Masters Tournament, played there since 1934. The Augusta National is a course known for open spaces, lush, smooth fairways, and multi-colored flowers. Designed by Alister Mackenzie, at the behest of past champion Bobby Jones, Augusta is a beautiful garden, where different fruit trees and flowers are planted at each hole. In fact, every hole is named after a flower. Thousands of azalea bushes, of 30 different varieties, are scattered throughout the course, where, at the beginning of the twentieth century, stood a fruit tree orchard. Every hole conjures up history and former players, but the most famous spot is Amen Corner, a trio composed of the 11th, 12th and 13th holes. There is no doubt that the most difficult hole is the 11th, as shown by the averages calculated at the end of each tournament.

248 LEFT The 9 holes of the par 3 Contest at Augusta National, seen from above.

248 RIGHT The white clubhouse, whose profile is reproduced on the trophy awarded to the winner of the Masters.

248-249 The home of the Masters occupies an area that was once a large orchard.

250-251 South African Trevor Immelman plays the 10th green during the 2008 Masters.

251 The 7th green, surrounded by bunkers.

252-253 The 12th green and the Ben Hogan Bridge. Several bridges at Augusta National are dedicated to past champions.

253 The 18th tee, also known as the "Holly," where players must overcome a prohibitive, narrow, corridor of trees to reach the green.

254-255 AND 255   The 7th hole at Pebble Beach reaches out into the Pacific Ocean in a stunningly beautiful natural landscape.

Pebble Beach
Golf Links

$\mathcal{P}$ebble Beach is always perfect, in spite of the warm California sun, when the white bunkers contrast with the gray rocks and green, smooth fairways. The front nine holes wind through the interior, while the back nine are aligned along the Pacific, which blows winds that make the course challenging, but fun. "If I only had one more round to play, I would choose to play it at Pebble Beach. I've loved this course from the first time I saw it. It's possibly the best in the world," said Jack Nicklaus. Since its inception in 1919, the stunning beauty of the course and the surrounding nature has intrigued and captured the heart of anyone who has visited it. Not only for the intriguing design by Jack Neville and Douglas Grant, but also because the location of the course is almost surreal. The back nine are near the ocean and, under the fairways, near rocks and the beach, thousands of seals, sea lions and penguins make their voices heard, while fearless squirrels, deer and fawn watch the silent phases of the game.

256-257 AND 257 At Cypress Point, the holes are carved from the cliffs and the ocean.

Cypress Point Club

$\mathcal{D}$riving the 17 Mile Drive, the road between Monterey and Carmel, California, you see many golf courses. Among them is the most inaccessible — a security guard at the entrance of the club forbids entry to non-members — Cypress Point, an almost unparalleled gem with many holes overlooking the Pacific Ocean. Hundreds of cypress trees dot the holes and some beautiful specimens can be found along the fairways. Less famous than the neighboring Pebble Beach, Cypress Point is unique for its relatively unmanicured ruggedness, which embraces the wildness of nature. Here too, the rocks play a big role and the wind gives a hard time to players who, in this case, are strictly members only.

The Ocean Course
Golf Course

𝒯he Ocean Course at Cabo del Sol in Mexico is a heady mix of sea and golf. Designed by the great Jack Nicklaus, it is in a dream location. The course is smooth, balanced and follows the natural undulations of the land, and, more than a mile of it stretches along a coastline of craggy rock outcrops and sun-drenched beaches. This award-winning 18-hole course is one of the few courses in the world that offers views of mountains, deserts and sea all in one place. Located on the tip of the Baja California peninsula, 19 ml (30 km) along the corridor between Cabo San Lucas and San Jose del Cabo, the Ocean Course is the second course designed by Nicklaus in Mexico. Hovering over a beautiful background, its emerald green grass contrasts with the blue Sea of Cortez. Praised by Nicklaus for the "three most beautiful holes of golf," the Ocean Course is surrounded by a natural desert landscape, with giant cacti that dominate the perfectly manicured greens and tees.

258 AND 258-259 The holes of the Ocean Course are surrounded by sand, desert, sea, and raw, wild vegetation. The result is infinitely scenic and visually striking.

The Fascination with Golf's Great Players

HARRY VARDON

Harry Vardon was a great, world-class, player throughout his career which began in 1896, when he won his first Open Championship, at Muirfield. He would win five more, the last at Prestwick in 1914 before it was suspended until 1920 because of WWI. In 1920, Vardon was 50 but still he almost won the U.S. Open at the Inverness Golf Club in Toledo, Ohio. He came second to Edward "Ted" Ray.

His most important legacy, however, was the "Vardon Grip" that every golfer uses today. It was Vardon who invented and perfected the grip and it has remained unchanged for more than a century. Born on 9 May 1870, on the Channel Island of Jersey, Vardon was the son of a gardener, and the fifth of seven children. The beautiful island enjoys a mild climate, and was frequented by many wealthy English tourists, who brought golf with them. Serving as a caddy, the young Harry understood, early on, that he liked golf and was able to play it well. At age 17 he was sent to serve as a gardener for an army major who happened to love golf but didn't like having a partner as clever and capable on the fairway as Harry was. Vardon soon received some balls and clubs as a gift, which brought out his true ability. The leading golf expert at the time, Horatio Hutchinson, reported that Vardon used shorter and lighter clubs than other players but still hit drives of extraordinary length and accuracy. Often, in fact, he played with borrowed clubs, frequently preferring those made for women. In 1900 an American businessman offered Harry the chance of a year-long overseas tour. He would soon become very popular in America because he won every match except one. When he showed up at the U.S. Open, and won it, his fame soared to new heights. Back in Britain, he was a wealthy champion, but, unfortunately, tuberculosis forced him to take a long stay in a sanatorium and put his career on hold, but he soon bounced back.

WALTER HAGEN

Born in Rochester, New York, in 1892, Walter Hagen is remembered as one of the most extroverted characters in golf, a sport which he helped to modernize. His achievements, including four Open Championships, two U.S. Opens and five U.S. PGA Championships, seemed less important than the show that Hagen would stage at every tournament. Hagen was the first golfer to embrace the commercial possibilities offered by various golf-related products. His bag, for example, contained 22 clubs instead of 14 because he was being paid $500 per year for each club he used. At the height of his popularity, he was also paid large sums to participate in competitions and exhibitions.

At the time, however, professionals were considered to be on the lowest rung of the golfing ladder, especially in Britain. Usually, they were not allowed to use the club facilities where they played, and, in many cases, were also even forbidden the use of the front door. On one occasion, he parked his Rolls Royce in front of the entrance to a clubhouse and used the car as a dressing room and restaurant. On another occasion, he refused to enter a clubhouse to collect a prize because he had been refused entry prior to the tournament.

His ability was not result of meticulous mental or physical preparation. As a player, his form was either absolutely wonderful or absolutely dreadful. Luckily he was a master of the recovery shot. Hagen was one of the first players to use psychology against his opponents. He once called an opponent out of a clubhouse to watch him sink a putt on the 18th and told him that the next day he would beat him and win the tournament – which he did. He was also the mainstay of the American Ryder Cup team from 1921 to 1935, and the non-playing captain in 1937.

Hagen was quite familiar with members of the British royal family. He counted future kings, Edward, Prince of Wales and George, Duke of Kent, among his friends. On one occasion, Hagen asked Edward to hold the flag, and the future king obliged without batting an eyelid. After one Open Championship, a photograph was being taken of the two princes with all of the participating players seated behind them. When Hagen arrived, he asked for another chair, placed it between the future kings and sat down. It was the nature of the man and the right place for a prince of golf.

chapter five

BOBBY JONES

"The Legend of Bagger Vance" is the story of a challenge match (which probably never took place) between two champions from the past – Walter Hagen and Robert Tyre Jones Jr., a young, wealthy and intelligent American who everyone called Bobby (despite the fact that he disliked the nickname). In any sport it is difficult to make comparisons between players of different eras. The same is true with golf and Bobby Jones but, up to now, no other player has been able match his Grand Slam win in 1930.

In1923, he won his first U.S. Open. It was like opening a dam – for seven years afterwards even the best professionals were unable to beat this young amateur. Every year he won at least one national title, winning 13 out of 21 tournaments in which he participated. In 1927, at St. Andrews, he declared that if he won, it would clear the inglorious failure from six years earlier, and he would leave the cup at the club. Those words won the hearts of the people of St. Andrews, who showed him affection and respect, transforming Robert Tyre Jones Jr. into the most popular American in Britain. This Affection would last a lifetime and beyond. In 1930, at the height of his golfing career, and at age 28, Bobby Jones retired from competition. The news surprised many, who felt that it was bolt from the blue. The fact was that Bobby Jones was only a golfer for four months of the year and spent the other eight months working in the family law firm. However, Bobby Jones devoted more time to golf after he stopped being a player. Spalding helped him create the first set of 14 clubs, and, with Warner Bros., he produced a series of short films entitled "How to play golf." But, most remarkable of all, he gave birth to the Augusta National. With the help of Alister Mackenzie, the golf architect, he built an 18 hole course within the orchard's 148 acres, naming each hole after a flowering and/or aromatic tree or shrub. In this way, the Masters tournament was born, allowing Jones to catch up with his professional friends at least once a year.

SAM SNEAD

Samuel Jackson Snead, from Ashwood, Virginia, is one of the greatest characters in world golf simply because of the number of his PGA Tour victories – 81. In fact, he won more tournaments than any other professional golfer. Snead won all of the biggest events in the world except one – the U.S. Open. Snead won the PGA Championship and the Masters three times, he also won the Open Championship at St. Andrews in 1946 and participated in the Ryder Cup eight times, twice as captain.

Snead came to golf literally by accident when, at age 15, having gained some attention as a football player, he broke his hand during an especially rough game. The injury was serious enough to end his football career, and he so he devoted himself to golf. In 1934, three professionals showed up and asked Sam to show them the ins and outs of the course. After a few holes they saw who they were dealing with. He finished the round in 61 and the news caused a sensation, with some wealthy members suggesting that he try to go professional. He would soon qualify for the Tour and win his first Open, at Oakland, in his first appearance. In the same year he showed that he had adapted well to this harsh world by winning four tournaments and finishing second at the U.S. Open for the first time. Interestingly, he was the first to wear the legendary green jacket destined for the winner of the Masters. The first Masters, in 1934, had been won by Horton Smith, but it was not until 1949 that the Green Jacket was attached to the trophy. When he turned 70, in 1982, the images of his 70-stroke round made headlines across the country. What better way to celebrate his birthday? Snead was also known to enjoy betting, although he never risked much when putting his money on the line. After all, he had written a book called "How to always win at golf."

GARY PLAYER

At less than five feet seven inches and 150 pounds, Gary Player is the "Black Knight." He is one of the "Big Three", the great players who made golf so exciting during the 1960s and 1970s, in the process earning themselves the nickname "The Modern Triumvirate." Along with Jack Nicklaus and Arnold Palmer, he played a part in many duels. His personal nickname, meanwhile, had been awarded at the beginning of his career because of his habit of playing in black pants, black hat and black t-shirt, saying that this color would attract all the energy of the sun that a lighter color would only reflect back. The sun helped him do remarkably well in nine Majors, 21 victories on the PGA Tour and 23 on the Senior Tour. A total of 163 around the world. Given his diminutive physique, he was the first player in the world to train his body in an almost maniacal way. Born in Johannesburg on 1 November 1935, he won his first Open at age 21.

At the beginning of his career, Player often crossed paths with another great South African, Arthur D'Arcy "Bobby" Locke. Player was known for taking strict daily sessions in the gym, and following a very challenging diet; these were the secrets of his success, which he maintained until the 1990s. This discipline is perhaps the reason for his longevity. Gary Player is, in fact, the only player in the world to have won the Open Championship in three different decades.

Once he joined the Senior Tour, he continued to be successful, but his time was now divided between the game and many other activities. He is a great designer of courses and has made them throughout the world, but his great passion is horse racing, and, in order to breed horses, he bought a large farm near Johannesburg.

ARNOLD PALMER

Every sport has a supreme player who transforms the game from a pastime to an art form, a person who attracts public attention by his mere presence. In the world of golf, that person is Arnold Palmer. Arnold Palmer is many things to many people – an immortal, world-class, golfer, a successful businessman, a prominent advertising spokesman, a skilled aviator, a talented golf course designer (he's designed over 100 around the world), consultant to the Golf Channel, a family patriarch, owner of Bay Hill and Latrobe Golf and part of an investment group involved in Pebble Beach. American to the core, Palmer, nevertheless, has some English blood in his veins, as his ancestors probably emigrated from England in 1780, settling in Latrobe, Pennsylvania. Arnold's father started Arnold's career almost by accident. Growing up with his father's teachings, he didn't have much style but knew how to hit the ball, growing up with a personalized swing that made him unique in the world, especially when finishing.

When he decided to turn professional, he understood that an important part of being a man in the public eye was to please the spectators, which he has always tried to do. This is why Arnold Daniel Palmer has become the most popular golfer in history. In addition to his magnificent performance record and his magnetic personality, his inexhaustible kindness, generosity and concern for all those with whom he comes into contact have endeared him to millions around the world and many have joined "Arnie's Army."

Even today, he is one of those players that still makes the most money in the world. As a young man he often played with a lawyer friend, Mark McCormack, who was good but not good enough to become a professional. He loved golf, and convinced Arnold to entrust him with the management of his interests as a player. McCormack soon proved himself an expert at managing contracts, and, in 50 years, Palmer not only proved to be a great player, but a real businessman. The springboard that launched him to fame and fortune was his victory at the U.S. Amateur Championship in 1954 – he would become a professional a few months later. His hottest period was between 1960 and 1963, when he captured 29 titles and collected almost $400,000 at a time when compensation was miniscule compared with today's earnings. In 1959 he won his first Major, the U.S. Open, and in 1961 and 1962 he won the Open Championship. In all, he won 60 victories on the U.S. Tour, and about 30 around the world, from Australia to Paris.

JACK NICKLAUS

Jack Nicklaus won 73 PGA Tour events in his career. Only one player has won more. But will anyone beat his record of 18 Majors? His beginnings were not easy. He was born in Columbus, Ohio, in January 1940, the burly boy found his escape on green meadows where, from age 14, he was practically unbeatable. Yet, at University he was still called "Fat Boy" and it was only after turning professional and enjoying success that he became universally known as the "Golden Bear."

Nicklaus won the U.S. Amateur Championship in 1959 and 1961. Jack was rightly proud of these victories, and, like the great Bobby Jones, likened them to victories in Majors. He became a professional in 1962, earning just $33 for his first event. But things improved quickly, and he won his first Major that same year by beating Palmer in an 18 hole playoff at the U.S. Open. At age 26, Nicklaus had completed the Grand Slam. Then, he won it all again, for a second time. And, finally, by winning the 1978 Open Championship, he had won all three of them three times each. His last success was important. In 1986, at age 46, he won his sixth Masters. His records are almost endless, but we should mention a few. He participated in 154 consecutive Majors, from the 1957 U.S. Open to the 1998 U.S. Open, and, for 17 consecutive years, he was in the top ten of the U.S. Money List, winning at least one tournament every year.

Like most of the champions of his generation, even the 'Golden Bear' has many other interests in the world of golf. He has, in fact, become a successful businessman, with hundreds of companies involved in the design of golf courses, the production of clothing and equipment and the management of many Golf Academies. He is also involved in the management of a race course, a factory and the production of fine wines.

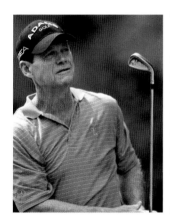

TOM WATSON

Tom Watson did not win the 2009 Open Championship at Turnberry, which could have allowed him, at age 59, to equal the record of six Open victories, belonging to Harry Vardon. Between 1977 and 1983 (when he was between the ages of 28 and 34), Tom Watson was considered virtually unbeatable. Up until 1975, Watson had earned a reputation for not being able to withstand the pressure of the final round in tournaments. Dramatically, in his early career, he had lost three Majors in the final round. Most other players would have been devastated but Tom Watson just wanted to understand why it was happening. Helping him find the reason for these collapses was Byron Nelson, who suggested relaxing the knees and slowing down his swing when he felt tense.

In 1975, Watson took on the Open Championship at Carnoustie. He was 26, a doctor of psychology and a wonderful student at Stanford University. In fact, as a boy, he had been called "the Thinker." He came from Kansas City and was polite and elegant, even when, without apparent effort, he would send a drive 275 yds (250 m) down the middle of a fairway. With a persimmon driver and a steel shaft, he won at Carnoustie in a playoff. The days of crumbling in the final rounds were over. But the best was yet to come. In 1977, at Turnberry, Watson and Nicklaus played the famous "Duel in the Sun" at the Open Championship. Watson picked up another Masters victory in 1981, his second. The following year he won the only U.S. Open of his career at Pebble Beach, California, thanks to a chip shot that has gone down in the annals golfing history.

His failure to win his sixth Open Championship disappointed many fans, not only because of the non-victory, but because of how highly respected Watson was and is. In fact, shortly afterwards, Tom Watson was welcomed as an Honorary Member of the Royal & Ancient Golf Club of St. Andrews. Part of the reason behind this was that, despite his five Open Championships (Carnoustie, Turnberry, Muirfield, Troon, Royal Birkdale), he had never won at St. Andrews. These victories began in 1975 and continued in 1977, 1980, 1982 and 1983. In 1984, everyone hoped that Watson would win again, gathering his sixth crown in St. Andrews. But this time, Severiano Ballesteros stood in the way. Ballesteros would end up winning, and Watson would finish in second place, two strokes behind.

Even in the most blessed of lives, then, you can't have everything. Tom Watson, for example, shares a major failure with Arnold Palmer. Neither has ever won the U.S. PGA Championship.

GREG NORMAN

Born on 10 February 1955 in Australia, he began playing in 1971, and would become a scratch player just two years later. Greg Norman at first wanted to become an air force pilot. Golf came along by chance. His mother Toini was a good player, who competed in important tournaments. She needed a caddy that did not speak and did not want to give a point of view at critical moments. Her son, Greg, was perfect. He was a robust and sturdy 14-year old who knew nothing about golf, and, therefore, had no opinions or advice to give. But, watching his mother gave him the desire to play.

The 'laissez faire' attitude that colored the start of his career may have been more of a character trait, one that may have played a part in his tendency to crumble in final rounds. It's a familiar story. On the last hole of a tournament which Norman thinks is in the bag, something suddenly happens to give the victory to an opponent he had thought was dead in the water. This scenario, over the years, has been played out more than thirty times. Just recall the 1996 Masters. Greg Norman began the final round with a six-stroke lead over Nick Faldo. Faldo won, by cutting into those six strokes slowly but surely. At the 1986 U.S. PGA Championship, Norman lost the cup because Bob Tway sank a shot from the bunkers, and the following year at the Masters, Norman lost a playoff against Larry Mize because Mize was able to produce a truly unique chip shot.

By the end he had amassed 86 victories – 20 on the PGA Tour and 66 around the rest of the world. Norman would end up being the first player to earn 12 million dollars on the PGA Tour, which would more than double after endorsements, and his income from investments as manager of Great White Shark Enterprises, a company that deals with golf courses, clubs and clothing.

Called the "White Shark" by an American journalist during the 1981 Masters, he was already quite aggressive. Over the next 20 years, the world would find out just how aggressive. He was enrolled in the World Golf Hall of Fame in 2001.

PAYNE STEWART

The U.S. Open Championship, the tournament that crowns champions, is staged in mid-June every year. The courses, on which the best golfers in the world compete, change every year, with a tendency to rotate. The second course at Pinehurst is one of the most famous, thanks to the second and final victory of Payne Stewart in 1999. He won his first U.S. Open at Hazeltine, Minnesota. In 1999, Stewart faced Phil Mickelson, who was desperate to finally win a Major. It had been one of the most competitive finals in U.S. Open history and it all came down to the final putts. The crowd, who had stopped breathing, erupted into rapturous applause when he won.

Payne Stewart had been a familiar figure to many people. From his father he inherited a taste for tartan fabrics and bright colors. He realized that he could stand out from other players by focusing on what he wore. In 1982, Stewart, who was born in 1957, in Springfield, Missouri and had been a professional since 1979, appeared for the first time in public wearing his famous lavender "plus four" pants. This was a big hit with the crowds, who approved of his unique style. It was something he could not give up. Payne Stewart was introduced to golf at age four by his father William, a good amateur himself who had won some prestigious titles. His father would teach him respect for the game and for his opponents, both on and off the fairway. 1999 began with a victory at Pebble Beach in February, followed by a second place in the Honda Classic, and then another in the MCI Classic. Then, on 20 June, he won his second U.S. Open. Then fate dealt a cruel blow to a happy man of 42, who only a few weeks earlier had shown his exceptional ability. The champion died in a plane crash, on 25 October 1999, while flying on a private Learjet from Orlando to Dallas to inspect land for a new course. The small plane lost cabin pressure and all five passengers died instantly.

BERNHARD LANGER

Bernhard Langer was one of the most talented golfers the world had ever seen. An American citizen since 2001, he had been born in Anhausen, Germany, in 1957. At age eight, the small Bernhard had followed in his brother's footsteps and become a caddy at the Augsburg golf club, about six miles from home. He had been a sickly child who had been taken under the wing of a top local player, who, for six years, had taught him the ropes. At age 14, Bernhard managed to get hired as an assistant teacher at the Monaco Golf Club. It was a financially secure position, but one Langer would have done for free as the work meant he could continue to train under the supervision of an expert, Heinz Freiburg, who had already figured out that the boy was endowed with natural ability.

He really came to the public's attention at age 17, when he won the 1974 German Open. Jan Brugelman was a man passionate about golf. He watched the young Bernhard with great interest, and was amazed that a boy with no real experience could win the tournament, surprising everyone. Brugelman asked him if he would accept financial aid, in what today would be more or less a sponsorship deal. Langer quickly made a name for himself with three victories in America and two at the Masters and he picked up 63 other victories around the world. He did this in 27 seasons, beginning in 1976, which, according to the official statistics of the European PGA Tour, averages out to be two wins every year. Langer built his career by always looking forward. In 1976 he joined the European Tour Order of Merit in 90th place. Two years later he had already moved up to 40th. Two years after that he had reached 9th and was at the top by 1981. He won the Australian Masters, the Casio World Open in Japan, the Million Dollar at Sun City – seven tournaments on five continents, and one year he even ended up in first place in the world rankings. In 27 years, he won over 44 million dollars in prize money.

Today, he is settled in Florida, where there is good weather, good schools for children, and, of course, beautiful golf courses, where someone can train quietly and purposefully.

NANCY LOPEZ

Most great golfers start playing at around the age of eight. Among them is the sensational Nancy Lopez, who was born on 6 January 1957. In 1998 she retired from competition after 25 years of almost continuous success – 48 wins and three women's Majors. Only the Women's U.S. Open eluded her. Her family is of Mexican origin, and Marina, her mother, is the hub of the whole story. Doctors diagnosed her with a pulmonary dysfunction and suggested that she take long walks outdoors. She and her husband decided to take up golf and would bring young Nancy along to the course when they played and allow her to hit a few balls.

It did not take them long to realize that Nancy had natural talent. Domingo, her father, understood that his daughter was meant for a fate better than his. He put all the family resources into making sure she was able to develop her game. Her parents realized that their daughter's career meant incurring some expenses so they started saving. These sacrifices, however, soon paid off. On 22 June 1977, at age 19, she turned professional. She finished the following year with a series of victories. In all, she won eight competitions, including five in a row. She also won the LPGA Rookie of the Year and Player of the Year awards. After that, things only got better. She managed to beat the records of her competitors. The great Judy Rankin, in 1976, had established annual earnings of $150,000. In 1978 Nancy ended the year with $200,000. With children from two marriages, seeing her on the course with two kids and two nannies became a familiar sight. She was to be rewarded for this determination in 1987 when she was enrolled in the LPGA Hall of Fame. This was in recognition for her 35 official tournament wins and a decade of good play on the tour.

NICK FALDO

For several years Nick Faldo has been considered the best English (and maybe European) golfer. Rightly, he was given one of the sport's most prestigious tasks – 2008 Ryder Cup captain. The job of captain is not only athletic, it also requires a total investment of experience, psychology, strategy, and tactics. And, fittingly, few people in the world have the same amount of Ryder Cup experience as that accumulated by Nick Faldo during his lifetime as an extraordinary player. One could even say that Severiano Ballesteros (a victorious captain at Valderrama in 1997) is not his equal. On the evening of 11 April 1971, the young Nicholas Alexander Faldo, born in Welwyn Garden City on 18 July 1957, could not sleep. Welwyn Garden City is a pleasant town in Hertfordshire, about thirty miles north of London. At that time, however, there was not much for a boy of 14 to do but watch television. So that was what he did. That evening the Masters in Augusta was being broadcast. He tuned in just as Jack Nicklaus was pulling a five iron from his bag. The flight of the resulting shot was very high, and it seemed to get lost in the sky, before falling on the green, just beyond the flag. It stopped for a second, vibrating, before rolling backwards towards the hole. The crowd went wild. Nick spent all his free time practising. On some evenings, his hands would be bleeding after more than a thousand swings. Nick had many interests, but he only ever thought about golf. At that point, he won a scholarship to the University of Houston, Texas, but after just two months, he could be heard saying, "We study too much here, I don't have time for the driving range." At age 19, he returned home and became a professional golfer. We now know that he had made a good choice, because in the end Faldo won three Masters and three Open Championships. In the midst of these victories, in 1984, he stopped suddenly, and sought out the help of David Leadbetter, who helped him reassemble his swing. This is an example of one of his most outstanding character traits – he is a perfectionist.

SEVERIANO BALLESTEROS

He exploded on to the golf scene. It was he who first broke many of the unwritten rules among professionals. Who would have thought that this introverted Spaniard – with a very long name – could conquer the hearts of golf fans? Born on 9 April 1957 into a poor family, he learned to play close to home, on the beach, with a three-iron and a ball given to him by a caddy at the nearby Santander golf club. Ballesteros was raised in a family of golfers. His three brothers were professionals, and an uncle, Ramon Sota, finished sixth in the 1965 Masters. Severiano joined the Tour at age 18, accompanied by his brother Manuel, who was also a professional.

Severiano Ballesteros was often considered to be the Arnold Palmer of Europe. A charismatic, beautiful, elegant, and bold player, who had the courage to risk everything to achieve the impossible and whose star power elevated the European Tour to new levels by helping Europe achieve equality – indeed, superiority – in the Ryder Cup. Creativity, imagination and short-game brilliance were the hallmarks of the Ballesteros game. He could miss the fairway off the tee, but at his best, would rarely encounter any problems.

In 1978, Ballesteros won for six consecutive weeks on three different continents. With the 1979 Open Championship, he obtained the first of his five Majors. The next was the 1980 Masters, however, he was disqualified from the U.S. Open that same year because he had arrived late at a tee. In 1983 he won the Masters again, and in 1988 the Open Championship, celebrating with his arm in the air. This would become a trademark in 1984, distinguishing the clothing company and design firm, which produced and organized golf courses and golf events, that he had founded.

Ballesteros dominated the European Tour until the early 1990s (50 victories on the European Tour, six on the PGA Tour, and participation in eight Ryder Cups) and brought Europe its first great achievements in the Ryder Cup. He will be remembered as the "Captain" for the commitment, dedication, support and promotion given to the event which, for the first time, was held in mainland Europe, at Valderrama in Spain. The great European champion died on May 7, 2011.

COLIN MONTGOMERIE

Golf has some unique characters. There are players who win everything, and oxygen at the top of the rankings fills their lungs for their entire careers. There are those who know how to reverse fate – authors of unbelievable comebacks. Then there is a small group who set the standards for professionalism. Consistently very good, and capable of great performances, they somehow never really excel. The best player in Europe, for example, has never won a Major. His name is Colin Montgomerie, and he is the captain of the European Ryder Cup team.

Montgomerie was born in 1963, in Glasgow, Scotland, to a middle class family. Starting young, it was understood early on that the boy had the right stuff, aided by the presence his mentor, Bill Ferguson. Montgomerie's story, however, is both easy and difficult to tell, in the sense that his career seems to have been that of a gentleman, dotted with interludes of golf. This has to do with his elegant playing style, which gives the impression that he does not like to be rushed. He became a professional in 1987, at age 24, after having shown himself to be the best amateur in Scotland. He put on a display in the 1989 Portuguese Open by setting a course record of 63. In the meantime, he won the Scandinavian Masters, the Dutch Open and the Volvo Masters, making four 'holes in one', and receiving the Vardon Trophy. In 1993, he became the top-ranking player in the Volvo Order of Merit, a position which he was to hold until 1999.

Since 1995, he has racked up a series of victories, but never in a Major. Fate, as they say, is a fickle mistress. And though sometimes Montgomerie can look like he's frowning, it's only because he's come to expect more from life and from himself.

PHIL MICKELSON

Phil Mickelson was a child prodigy. His father was a very good golfer and he would take his son to the club with him every time he played, and, when Phil was only eighteen months, and his father could no longer resist, he cut a club down to size and took him to a practice course to give him his first lesson. He stood his son in front of him, and not alongside him. Phil watched and began to imitate his father. Thus was born the first involuntary case of a false left-hander in the history of golf, because Phil is not left-handed. He does everything with his right hand. At age three and a half, he played his first 18 hole, par three, course at the Presidio Hills Golf Club, in San Diego, where he had been born on 16 June 1970. At age 14 his parents offered him a week's coaching at a Golf Digest school, where Dean Reinmuth, the great master, immediately spotted the great potential of the boy and ended up becoming his coach for many years. Careers, as you can imagine, are built little by little. The young Phil, however, came into the spotlight very soon.

By age 20, he had already made a name for himself. Adding to his collection of local prizes and awards, he won the 1990 U.S. Amateur with a second round of 64, and was invited, as an amateur, to play the Tucson Chrysler Classic. It was not easy, but he managed to win it. When he turned professional, in 1992, fans did not have to wait long to see him succeed, as he soon won many tournaments, including the Buick Invitational back home in San Diego. He had been creating an image for himself as a great player, with a certain style, but this was betrayed by his failure at the last hole. His inability to win a Major, however, had become part of his charm. Modern day fans may come to see Tiger Woods, but they're rooting for Mickelson, for this American boy with his beautiful wife Amy (who takes care of his website) and caddy "Bones" Mackay. He managed to win his first Major in 1994, at Augusta, unlocking a mental block. Now he's up to four Majors.

ANNIKA SÖRENSTAM

Annika came from a middle-class Swedish family. Her parents were both excellent golfers, especially her mother Gunilla. Annika, however, began by playing tennis. By age nine, she was already among the top ten juniors in Stockholm. She became so good, in fact, that she couldn't find any competition of her own age, and at age 12, decided to give up tennis and concentrate on golf. When Annika was in her twenties she moved to Arizona, having earned a college scholarship. She had just started to get attention in Sweden and was considered a nice acquisition for the university team. Since 1987, in fact, she had been a part of the Swedish Women's national team and, upon moving to the US, had to divide her time between the two. Upon graduation, she turned professional and struggled for two years, between 1990 and 1992. In 1993, she participated in three LPGA events. Soon, she joined the LPGA tour, and became one of its most important players. She achieved her first success in Australia, at the Holden Open, shortly afterwards attending her first Solheim Cup and the LPGA Tour named her Rookie of the Year. By the end of 1995, she was not only top of the European Money List, but also top of the American Money List too. The reason was that she had won the OVB Damen Open in Europe, for the first time, and, in America, recorded a victory at the Women's U.S. Open. By age 25 she was already in golf's history books. The reason for Annika Sorenstam's success, however, was quite simple – hard work. All players train a lot, but Annika never stops. She spends most of her time practising every day. Cycling, swimming, weight-lifting and kickboxing. This is Annika's secret. A schedule of extremely precise exercise and training. Annika has had a career that is difficult to compare with other athletes. The closest comparison on the men's side would be Tiger Woods, but this isn't really accurate. She has twice won the Women's U.S. Open, and was the first woman to hit a 59 (31 +28). She has won in Hawaii, Australia, half of Europe, Japan, and many times has deserved the Athlete of the Year award in both her own country and America.

TIGER WOODS

The best, it was said until recently, was Tiger Woods, an unrivaled champion since 1997, the year in which he changed the face of golf. Woods won with a regularity that had very few precedents. Even as an amateur, he was one of the best golfers ever seen up to that time. Tiger Woods is an absolutely unique personality.

By age two he had already appeared on television, on the Mike Douglas Show, a hugely popular program, where he had challenged Bob Hope to a putting duel. At that age he had already learned to move the putter and flash a smile that enchanted viewers, paving the way for his later popularity.

Woods learned to play golf by watching his father, who practised in his garage, using a net to catch the ball. Retired lieutenant colonel Earl Woods married a Thai woman named Kultida, whom he had met in Vietnam. They set up home in Cypress, California, naming their first son Eldrick (although he would soon be nicknamed "Tiger" in honor of one of his father's lieutenants). Tiger's passion for golf led Earl to start looking at things from the perspective of a coach, and he taught his son well. By age four, Tiger was playing at the Navy Golf Club, finishing the first nine holes in 48. At age ten, he came under the wing of instructor John Anselmo, in Huntington Beach, California. Tiger had all the techniques and he could already hit the ball around trees, adjusting the precision of shots within inches. John Anselmo stayed with Woods until Tiger started working with Butch Harmon, the decisive hand in the Woods phenomenon, at age 18. Everything began on 23 August 1993. Since then, and at least ten times a year, most especially during the week before a Major, student and teacher would meet at the Butch Harmon Golf Club in Las Vegas or in Isleworth, near Tiger's home in Florida. Tiger Woods has already won everything. He will always be a favorite. His goals appear to have been achieved, the successes now so numerous that his main challenger is himself, even if he still trails Jack Nicklaus in the number of Majors won (18) and PGA Tour victories (73), with Sam Snead (82) ahead of both of them.

LEE WESTWOOD

Born at Worksop, Nottinghamshire in 1973, this English boy had learned at a very young age, to handle the golf clubs his grandparents – and golf enthusiasts – had given him as a gift when he was thirteen. It had been love at first sight, and only two years later, he won the Junior Championship in his county. On the other hand, Lee had always been into sports. During his school years he excelled especially in cricket, rugby and football, which is his passion still today. After winning the British Youth Championship he turned pro in 1993 and in 1996 conquered the Scandinavian Masters, his first success. Throughout his career he has won 23 titles in the European Tour, other triumphs in each continent (two in the PGA Tour, in the St. Jude Classic and in 2000 he was awarded the European Order of Merit, putting an end to Montgomerie's domination. Subsequent to the three years in which he had suffered great technical setbacks he made an overwhelming comeback among the giants in 2007 and in 2009 won the Dubai World Championship, the first edition of the Race to Dubai, Portugal Masters and the European Order of Merit. On October 31,2010 he became the World Ranking's Number One. A rather strange and rare fact is that Westwood, despite his many wins, has never managed to win a Major even though, on a few occasions, he had come quite close to doing so, as in 2010, when he placed overall third in the US Open.

A strong point of the Ryder Cup challenge, Westwood participated in all the last seven editions, and became the event's attraction pole, priding himself in a very impressive record of 29 matches, 14 wins, 5 draws for a total of 16 and a half points gained for the team.

His life has been decisively set on golf and in fact he married Laurae Coltart, sister of Andrew, and begot two children and is the best friend of Darren Clarke his partner, with whom in 2006 he bought a private plane with which the two travel move about around Europe.

LORENA OCHOA

Lorena Ochoa was born on 15 November 1981 in Guadalajara, Mexico. She began playing, at age five, at the Guadalajara Golf Club, where her wealthy parents had been members for many years. Lorena was fond of golf, and a year later she won her first competition. By age eight, she had already won the World Junior Championship, in San Diego, California. Of course, by that time, she was also playing tennis at national level, and was considered to be among the great prospects of Mexican tennis. Lorena chose golf, but did not abandon other sports. She tried her hand at track and field, basketball, competitive swimming, and cycling, all while training for mountain biking in the summer and snowboarding in the winter. She was also interested in marathons. Muscular but well proportioned, Lorena exuded a rare level of energy and never stopped.

She turned professional in May 2002 and was hailed Rookie of the Year and Player of the Year. Lorena joined the LPGA tour in 2003 and rose to the top ten, with two second place results. She ended up ninth in the Money List that year. 2004 was even better. She earned her first two Tour titles, the Franklin Championship (Lorena became the first Mexican golfer to win it on the women's tour), and the Wachovia LPGA Classic. By then it had become clear that she was comparable to the great stars of golf.

Her training schedule is punishing. Tons of putting and precise long-game practice and long hours in the gym. She is, to put it simply, a golf machine. In 2005 she played in 20 competitions, winning one and finishing second on four occasions, with ten other top ten results. In 2006, she earned six victories, six second places, and 20 top ten results. Here are a few figures to put her success in perspective – in 2007, until late August, she participated in 19 competitions, with six wins, four second places, one third, and 16 top ten placements. But that's not all – on 23 April 2007, she took over the world number one ranking from Annika Sorenstam. But that still was not enough. On 5 August 2007, on the Old Course at St. Andrews, Lorena won the Women's British Open.

AUTHOR

Maria Pia Gennaro was born a golfer long before she became a journalist. Though her studies were not in the field of journalism, she chanced upon this career path and turned her passion into her trade. She began writing just before her 20th birthday, almost as a joke, but she progressed quickly and worked at Parliamo di Golf for nine years, followed by Golf News and Tee Shot. She then moved on to Golf & Turismo from 2007 to 2010. In 2011 she became the editor in chief of Golf Today. She's covered more international tournaments than any specialty journalist in Italy. Her frequent presence in press rooms around the world led to an invitation to join the Association of Golf Writers. After collaborating on a volume for the Menaggio & Cadenabbia Golf Club centennial, she wrote about the history of the Varese and Bologna clubs. She then went on to outline the text and choose the images for Omaggio al Golf (published by Mondadori).

INDEX

PHOTO CREDITS

The Publisher would like to thank Gaston and Christian Barras,
and the Golf Club Crans-sur-Sierre for their helpful collaboration

The Publisher also wishes to thank:
Stuart McEwen (Kingsbarns Golf Links), Yves Dewaegenaere (Turnberry Golf Course), Vari McGreevy (Ballybunion Golf Club),
Berthold Apel (Hamburger Golf-Club), Norman Vickery (Les Bordes), Manuela Whittaker (Landmrk Media),
Umberto Rissone (Royal Park I Roveri), Aaron Newnham (Royal Melbourne Golf Club),
Lynne J. Davis and Ryan Brandeburg (Cape Kidnappers), Elisabetta Mazzei (Fairmont Banff Springs),
Ryan Pierce (Pebble Beach), Branden Hanson (Cypress Point), Larry Lambrecht (Ocean Course).

WHITE STAR PUBLISHERS

WS White Star Publishers® is a registered trademark
property of Edizioni White Star s.r.l.

© 2011 Edizioni White Star s.r.l.
Via M. Germano, 10
13100 Vercelli, Italy
www.whitestar.it

Translation: Salvatore Ciolfi
Editing: Norman Gilligan

ISBN 978-88-544-0603-2
1 2 3 4 5 6   15 14 13 12 11

Printed in Indonesia